AF065004

Romanti*k*
Journal for the Study of Romanticisms

Editors
Gísli Magnússon (University of Iceland), Benedikt Hjartarson (University of Iceland), Kim Simonsen (University of Amsterdam), Thor J. Mednick (University of Toledo), Marie-Louise Svane (University of Copenhagen), Marja Lahelma (University of Helsinki), and Sine Krogh (University of Aarhus)

Advisory Board
Charles Armstrong (University of Bergen), Jacob Bøggild (University of Southern Denmark, Odense), David Fairer (University of Leeds), Karin Hoff (Georg-August-Universität Göttingen), Stephan Michael Schröder (University of Cologne), David Jackson (University of Leeds), Christoph Bode (LMU Munich), Carmen Casaliggi (Cardiff Metropolitan University), Gunilla Hermansson (University of Gothenburg), Knut Ljøgodt (Nordic Institute of Art, Oslo), Paula Henrikson (Uppsala University), Dorthe Jørgensen (University of Aarhus), and Joep Leerssen (University of Amsterdam)

Romantik
Journal for the Study of Romanticisms

Volume 10|2021

V&R unipress

Contents

Foreword 7

Essay

Emil Månsson (University of Iceland)
Deadseeing and Its Discontents: A Critical Phenomenology of Ecocide
and Earthcare 13

Articles

Robert W. Rix (University of Copenhagen)
The Spectre Barber: Shaving the Ghost in the Eighteenth and Nineteenth
Centuries 37

Anthony Apesos (Lesley University)
Visionary Anatomy: Blake's Bodies 57

Sveinn Yngvi Egilsson (University of Iceland)
Territorial Kinship and the Feminine Land: Icelandic Patriotic Poetry in an
International Context 83

Helena Bergmann (University of Borås)
Cross-Channel Motions: The Educational Writings of Mary Hays Versus
Those of Pauline de Meulan-Guizot 105

Anne Jerslev (University of Copenhagen)
David Lynch and the Fragment 115

Review

Lea Grosen Jørgensen
Mythology and Nation Building: N. F. S. Grundtvig and His European Contemporaries. Edited by Sophie Bønding, Lone Kølle Martinsen, and Pierre-Brice Stahl 139

About the Authors 143

Foreword

At the Copenhagen Book Fair 2021, the scholar Aksel Haaning and author Josefine Klougart were interviewed by biologist Rasmus Ejrnæs.[1] At one point, Ejrnæs asks Haaning – an expert on hermeticism – if Paracelsus saw the destructive potential of nature or if he was just a romantic who thought that everything was good. Haaning answered that this was a parodic description of romanticism which echoed the criticism of idealism in the modern breakthrough during the last decades of the 19th century. Rather, the romantics saw nature as a cycle of creation and destruction, a unity of light and darkness, an idea inspired by Paracelsus. According to Haaning, we are just rediscovering what romanticism really was. At the end of the interview, Klougart returns to romanticism: 'It is interesting that there is so much resistance in our culture against seeing romanticism as a progressive period. In my opinion, it is very much so. I think the future is romantic!'[2] Spontaneously, Haaning and Klougart addressed questions about romanticism with which *Romantik – Journal for the Study of Romanticisms* is also concerned: Do we sufficiently understand the (esoteric or hermetic) roots of romanticism? Does the current of romanticism belong to the past or do certain elements of romanticism live on? Does the cultural criticism of romanticism offer better ways to engage with nature than the instrumental reduction of it to mere resources? In the interview itself, Klougart does not elaborate on these points, but she and Haaning are not alone in their appreciation of a romantic philosophy of nature which seeks to transcend a disenchanting and often harmful instrumental approach to it.

In a Danish context, the publishing house Forlaget Virkelig and the journal associated with it *Ny Jord – Tidsskrift for naturkritik* (*New Earth – Journal for Nature Criticism*) – founded by the poet and publisher Andreas Vermehren Holm – seem to hold a similar progressive view of romanticism. In the foreword of the second volume of *Ny Jord* in 2016, the editors wrote: '[…] certain writers and

---

1 https://www.radio4.dk/program/vildspor/?id=vildspor-live-fra-bogforum_ep_06_11_21.
2 My translation.

thinkers in romanticism and more generally in modernity offer a wealth of aesthetic and political forms and reflections on the relationship between man and nature and man *as* nature. If we begin to reconsider nature as a necessary part of critical thinking, we gradually challenge the categories of political and aesthetic thinking altogether.'[3] In this optic, romanticism appears as a both subversive political and visionary aesthetical way of thinking which is highly relevant even today. The authors published by Virkelig in many cases share an emphasis on re-enchantment and (often spiritual) appreciation of nature – one good example is *Ur-Geräusch* (Primal Sound) by the symbolist poet Rainer Maria Rilke, a short text which designates new, visionary ways of writing on the basis of a heightened synaesthetic awareness about nature.

If we widen the scope from a Nordic context, it is evident that romanticism has inspired scholars to think about philosophy of nature, environmentalism, ecology, and biology in new ways. To give just one example, Kate Rigby, a leading scholar within the field of environmentalist humanities, wrote a monograph with the telling title *Reclaiming Romanticism: Towards an Ecopoetics of Decolonization* where she seeks to bring romantic thought into the Anthropocene in an interdisciplinary way. She seeks to re-evaluate romanticism through a 'decolonial lens' and 'also draws on a range of other approaches within the wider field of the environmental humanities, including eco-religious studies, multispecies studies and bio-semiotics, in order to identify within romantic verse particular eco-poetic arts of resistance to hegemonic constructions of human subjectivity and instrumentalizing constructions of "nature".'[4] Rigby is, in other words, resorting to romanticism as a 'strategic recovery of European counter-traditions'.[5]

In the 2021-issue of *Romantik – Journal for the Study of Romanticisms*, we follow the path we laid out in the 2020 issue combining articles on the historical era of romanticism with attempts to show the continuous relevance of romantic thought up until our contemporary age. We, therefore, bring an essay by the young scholar Emil Månsson which is not explicitly about romanticism, but rather about a contemporary philosophy of nature which draws upon the romantic tradition of ascribing aliveness, value, and beauty to nature. The appreciation of nature, however, goes hand in hand with a criticism of modernity's 'deadseeing', as Månsson calls it. The result of the 'killing' of nature is the encompassing ecocide we are witnessing today. The essay is personal, maybe even polemical, but since it engages with the philosophical tradition (e. g. Husserl, Heidegger,

---

[3] Jeppe Carstensen, Peter Meedom, Sofie Isager Ahl, Ester Frish, Christoffer Basse Eriksen and Andreas Vermehren Holm (eds.), *Ny Jord – Tidsskrift for naturkritik 2* (2016), 5. My translation.

[4] Kate Rigby, *Reclaiming Romanticism: Towards an Ecopoetics of Decolonization* (London: Bloomsbury Academics, 2020), 4.

[5] Rigby, *Reclaiming Romanticism*, 189.

Chomsky), it also – indirectly – shows the potential for progressive romantic thought in our contemporary age.

In his article "The Spectre Barber: Shaving the Ghost in the Eighteenth and Nineteenth Centuries", Robert Rix focuses on the German folktale "Stumme Liebe" from the 'pre-Grimm' collection *Volksmärchen der Deutschen* (1782–1786) by Johann Karl August Musäus. According to Rix, the translation and retelling of the folktale in Britain led to negotiations of the supernatural, since Museäus had introduced satirical (debunking) elements to the oral story.

In the article "Visionary Anatomy: Blake's Bodies", Anthony Apesos explores the way in which William Blake's prints and drawings depict human anatomy. He demonstrates that Blake deviated from anatomical correctness as a subversive rejection of the mechanistic Newtonian world view.

In the article "Territorial Kinship and the Feminine Land: Icelandic Patriotic Poetry in an International Context", Sveinn Yngvi Egilsson compares the Icelandic tradition of patriotic poetry to the Danish one with which it shares certain structural characteristics: 1. An address to the country or the nation; 2. An enumeration of the typical characteristics of the country; 3. The use of common nouns, as opposed to proper nouns, since the poems are supposed to engage all Icelanders by using general descriptions of their country; 4. The confirmation of territorial kinship , i. e. the land as the parent or foster parent of each Icelander; 5. A wish, a prayer, a blessing, or a whetting on behalf of the country.

In the article "Cross-Chanel Motions: The Educational Writings of Mary Hays versus those of Pauline de Meulan-Guizot", Helena Bergmann seeks to investigate and compare two female educational writers from the romantic era, Mary Hays from Britain and Pauline de Meulan-Guizot from France. The writings of Mary Hays, a friend of Mary Wollstonecraft, were dedicated to the cause of female liberation. The works of Pauline de Meulan-Guizot were more focused on the moral upbringing of the young due to political concerns in the aftermath of the French Revolution. According to Bergmann, they shared, however, a deep concern for the future of the young in their respective societies.

In the article "David Lynch and the Fragment", Anne Jerslev demonstrates the fruitfulness of going back to the early romantic writers, in particular Friedrich Schlegel, in order to shed light on David Lynch's use of the fragment as an aesthetical device. According to Jerslev, it allows us to focus on the aesthetic surplus and affective atmosphere of the fragmented structure instead of traditional parameters such as coherence.

Lea Grosen Jørgensen reviews the anthology *Mythology and Nation Building: N. F. S. Grundtvig and His European Contemporaries* edited by Sophie Bønding, Lone Kølle Martinsen and Pierre-Brice Stahl. The anthology addresses the use of pre-Christian myths in European nation-building during the long 19th century, especially in the writings of N. F. S. Grundtvig (1783–1872), and according to

Grosen Jørgensen, 'the anthology handles its broad topics nationalism and mythology in a well-thought, comprehensive way, and its comparative method brings out new and overlooked aspects of well-known writers'.

Welcome to the 10th issue of *Romantik*.

Gísli Magnússon, on behalf of the editorial board

Essay

Emil Månsson
(University of Iceland)

Deadseeing and Its Discontents: A Critical Phenomenology of Ecocide and Earthcare

> *The reason our current system of material production kills the world is that it starts by seeing the world as dead. What then is there to love?*
> – Charles Eisenstein[1]

You can only kill what is alive. One way to characterise modernity, the age of ecocide on steroids that we call the Anthropocene, is to recognise a schismatic rift between those who take the world to be fundamentally dead, inert, and up for grabs – to be ultimately reducible to matter, whatever the finest ingredient may turn out to be – versus those who view the planet as essentially living and loveable. We might be inclined to distinguish between Moderns and Indigenous, but because skin colour and heritage doesn't completely determine a person's perception, even if it goes a long way towards shaping it, I call the former group 'deadseers' (after the concept of deadnaming) and the latter group 'planeteers' (after the 1990s cult TV show *Captain Planet and the Planeteers*). You may notice that deadseers speak of the world whereas planeteers see a living planet. This difference is already telling, but my main point is on a level apart, namely, that how you see, feel, and think the world/planet profoundly influences how you are and act in it, and it affects how you regard your own being and behaviour in it, which are of course two sides of a single coin. Are you a fair user or a nefarious abuser of the earth? Depending on the lens we view the world through, including the stories we tell ourselves, you may well be construed as either.

1. The Faults and Default of Deadseeing

Like the either unwitting or wanton act of 'deadnaming' a transgender person, i.e., calling them by their given name rather than their chosen name, deadseeing denotes the sometimes deliberately malevolent but oftentimes subliminal, habituated, and culturally and structurally sanctioned and sustained practice of *seeing reality in toto as fundamentally dead* – inert, indifferent, essentially reducible to fact and matter, to world-stuff or planet-thing. This is the prime mover

---

[1] Charles Eisenstein, *Climate: A New Story* (Berkeley: North Atlantic Books, 2018), 153.

and lingering ideology that *drives* environmental destruction, steering it and moving it forward. It's an eternal engine of ecocide; an ontological, hermeneutical, epistemic assault committed before any actual slaughter or pollution or deforestation, yet always already implicit in it. It motivates blind economism and legitimises unrestrained resourcism. It is, as it were, the original world war, World War Zero (WW0): A total, daily war on the world waged entirely out in the open, for all to see, yet so completely normalised and naturalised by most of us – though, importantly, not all of us – as to be rendered practically invisible.

The antithesis to deadseeing is the perception and appreciation that earthly reality is essentially alive. It is to see, which includes feeling and cognition, that the planet underfoot and overhead, outside as well as inside us, is teeming with relatives rather than resources. Some speak of such living earth perceptions in terms of animism or vitalism. Others prefer the rehabilitated term panpsychism, or the alternative panspiritism. Others again argue that we're seeing a rebirth of materialism, so they use the umbrella term new materialism. And finally, many take after David Abram in speaking of the more-than-human world, or worlds. Whatever label one might subscribe to, however, they all share in the basic perception and commitment that the earth is emphatically *not dead*, and see earthly reality as a sort of dialogical presence and partner with/in which human beings dwell and commune. And they agree that to see the world as alive is to naturally love and care for it, or it's at least a first step towards loving and caring. In any case, though, they – or, if I flatter myself, we – are vastly outnumbered.

The vices and wrongs that are attributable to the perceptual-attitudinal matrix that I call deadseeing are near endless. This is not exactly a good thing, and not just because the failings are bad in and of themselves, but because concepts that explain too much often explain very little. To define deadseeing, therefore, I need to confine it. I'm hesitant about this though. Part of its appeal to me is its immediate applicability and sweeping explanatory power. You should just see it and get it. Nevertheless, concepts necessitate conceptualisation. Or *storying.*

Deadseeing is the default perceptual mode of modernity. It is not only institutionalised but internalised by most people alive today, myself included. I still remember the shame when a girl I liked in elementary school found me lurking in a neighbourhood thicket, looking at birds! I knew intuitively that I shouldn't be. Only a child or a moron would have time for birds, and I didn't want her to see me as either. Of course I was a kid, and no doubt moronically in love, that's not the point (I don't recall my love interest's reaction, but I didn't get the girl; in fact, to see and speak of her as essentially obtainable is itself symptomatic of deadseeing). What stands out in my memory is this feeling of being caught in a for me utterly alien, unnatural, and somehow forbidden act of being with birds. How bizarre it seems to me today that I should have been ashamed at all. But also, when I think back on it, how good that something was calling or pulling me out there despite myself. I'm not sure my story is generalisable. All I know is that not too long ago I lived in a world where a boy was embarrassed to consort with blackbirds in-between Counter-Strike and Harry Potter. I am afraid I still live in that world.

Deadseeing, the concept, is my own invention. It has obvious parallels with the terms dehumanisation and objectification, but these classic terms are troubled in the ecological sense and context I use the term. Dehumanisation comes closest to the meaning I'm after, but that term clearly points to humans, so while there are ecophenomenological and animistic arguments for saying that the natural world is 'far more human than I once realised,' as Erazim Kohák writes in *The Embers and the Stars*, it makes for a roundabout argument against the default imposition of the empire of deadseeing.[2] As for the term objectification, there is both a mundane argument against it: that it lacks the gravity of dehumanisation, i.e., that it has been normalised; and there's a more technical argument, namely, that it upholds the subject-object distinction, and as such, the term's relevance is only implied as a negative, as the absence of subjectivity. Deadseeing, the name, retains the gravity of dehumanisation while dodging the dead-ends of that term, but at the same time refrains from reproducing an unhelpful dualism implied by objectification, when it's precisely not a matter of subjects vs. objects (or nature vs. culture, or some other unhelpful dichotomy), but of life and death (even if it is the exclusive domain of humans, and moreover, of some humans; and even if those 'some' in our days amount to most; in other words, even if the dichotomies of the human vs. non-human and the privileged vs. exploited remain, even so, it is first and foremost a matter of life and death).

Then there's depersonalisation, which like dehumanisation also captures the action of divesting someone or some*thing* of subjectivity, but without the explicit human focus. Still, within a worldview that already reserves personhood for the human animal, and perhaps degrees of personhood to some select other animals, depersonalisation also doesn't express the sheer enormity and severity involved in "naturally" stripping all or most of non-human nature not only of personhood but of basic aliveness. Deadseeing, we might therefore say, is depersonalisation *in extremis.*

Lastly, is deadseeing then a worldview? Whereas the latter notion denotes a comprehensive conception or apprehension of the world and human life therein, deadseeing designates the perceptual mode belonging to a particular worldview. Of course, the two cannot be thought apart; we may say that deadseeing makes the modern worldview tick. Moreover, because deadseeing so succinctly defines any worldview that equates reality with dead matter, I can see the word be used as a proxy for the overall worldview, especially given deadseeing's ocular focus,

---

2 Erazim Kohák, *The Embers and the Stars. A Philosophical Inquiry into the Moral Sense of Nature* (The University of Chicago Press, 1987), 90.

like worldview. Deadseeing, then, firstly names a conditioned, subconscious way of perceiving the world as fundamentally dead. But it may also, secondly, name the tacit entire worldview that that perceptual mode is born of and itself perpetuates.

Now, with this conceptual framework in place, we can return to the primary perceptual chasm between deadseers and planeteers.

2. Crisis Philosophy and the Task of Seeing

You can only kill what is alive – but surely what something is shouldn't depend on our representations of it? I don't know that this was ever true, but it is, I will claim, demonstrably false today, as evidenced best by our own species' ascent to geological force. Because we are the greatest geological mover, and because the havoc we wreak upon the planet is ultimately sanctioned and made possible by the way we narrate the world to ourselves, i. e., the way dominant culture views and projects the world, we cannot divorce worldview from world-building, the latter being, of course, equal parts construction and destruction, as we forever churn the living planet into dead empire.

In this sense, there is no reality behind or apart from the reality of our united yet so unequal despoiling of our home planet. Or rather, there is no other reality equally worth caring about and caring for. To quote Noam Chomsky's 1968 talk turned essay about the role of "Philosophers and Public Philosophy": 'A person who is not obsessed with this realization is living in a fantasy world.'[3] And more germanely, a thinking that is not obsessed with humanity's ecocidal and suicidal presence on Earth is no less fantastical, as in, removed from reality. Again with Chomsky, 'this task' – and here I unashamedly insert Eugen Fink's 1936 note to Husserl regarding 'the indispensable task of philosophy: humanity's responsibility for itself'[4] – this task, quote Chomsky, 'will be of greater human significance, for the foreseeable future, than the investigation of [say] the foundations of physics or the possibility of reducing mental states to brain states,'[5] regardless of the scientific benefit of said studies. All of which is merely to echo Chomsky's twin assertion that, 'in a time of crisis, one should abandon, or at least restrict, professional concerns that do not adapt themselves in a natural way toward the resolution of this crisis,' and that, 'There is no profession that can claim with

---

3 Noam Chomsky, "Philosophers and Public Philosophy," *Ethics* 79:1 (Oct. 1968), 2.
4 Edmund Husserl, *The Crisis of European Sciences and Transcendental Phenomenology. An Introduction to Phenomenological Philosophy* (Evanston: Northwestern University Press, 1970), Appendix X, 400 (Fink's outline for the continuation of the Crisis). Eugen Fink was Husserl's collaborator and research assistant from 1928 to 1938.
5 Chomsky, *Ethics*, 6.

greater authenticity [than that of philosophy] that its concern is the intellectual culture of the society or that it possesses the tools for the analysis of ideology and the critique of social knowledge and its use.'[6] If the end of the world – or in scarcely less dramatic terms, the mass dying of the natural world plus the human and more-than-human suffering that follow from it – does not warrant an all-hands-on-deck call to action and thinking, you shall surely be hard-pressed to find a worthier cause. And so, I consider these pages, and the literature they contribute to, *crisis philosophy.*

In fairness to Chomsky, he wasn't referring to universal bioannihilation and the ecological crisis when he wrote 50 years ago that we ought to be 'obsessed with this realization.' He was in fact commenting on the imperial-American violence in Asia during a single generation, from Japan 1942–45, to Korea 1950–53, to Vietnam 1965–68. Be that as it may, Chomsky's reality check is only that much stronger, and the text itself warrants our appropriation, I think, when taken as a comment on not just the American but the Anthropocene condition. And a second caveat: Chomsky is also not asking philosophers to assume the massive (not to mention megalomanic and/or impossible) burden of humanity's responsibility for itself, as loftily put forth by Fink. Chomsky, at least in 1968, only modestly suggests that philosophers take up 'the study of the technology of control and manipulation that goes under the name 'behavioral science' and that serves as the basis for the ideology of the 'new mandarins'[7] which is Chomsky's then-moniker for the American intellectual and technical classes whom he (i) asserts have seized power over universities and governments, the former furnishing the latter, and therefore (ii) holds accountable for much of American society's general failures, and for the Vietnam war atrocities in particular. That being said, it doesn't require an extraordinary perception to recognise that with the ascension and dissemination of neoliberal ideology after 1968,[8] the 'Neomandarinate', i. e. the reign of bureaucrats and managers and the economism they espouse, has but continued to grow and cement its position. And so, I will claim, this totalisation, which includes but isn't limited to globalisation, of the deadseeing management ideology (which Chomsky calls 'liberal technocracy') is itself sufficient to warrant our reading, namely, that the very same perceptual matrix that allowed for the American atrocities in Asia is what also permits the wholesale murder of our planet – and always has, and always will, unless something fundamentally gives – because this motor of assault mentality that I call deadseeing is neither new nor confined, but precisely total in every sense of the word: it is whole, absolute, all-

---

6 Chomsky, *Ethics,* 4–5.
7 Chomsky, *Ethics,* 6.
8 See for example Noam Chomsky's book published three decades after his 1968 talk turned article, *Profit Over People. Neoliberalism and Global Order* (New York: Seven Stories Press, 1998).

encompassing. There is no time or place it will not reach, no part of existence it cannot touch, nothing it will not subsume under its deadening gaze. And in case my appropriation of Chomsky's semi-century old text seems contrived, I will let his own words of late lend it further support: 'We are now facing a real existential crisis. The possibility that organised human life may continue on anything like the scale that we now know is very much threatened [...] So the task that is faced is not simply for climate scientists [...] but for everyone else to try to stop this race to disaster, which is not very far off in the distance.'[9]

The question is: How do we stop this race? Or, recalling Walter Benjamin's revision of Marx's analogy, how do we pull the brakes on this runaway train?[10] To ecophenomenologists (and according to many contemplative practises, I hasten to add), one must initially try to see and make sense. Not speculate or intuit, not calculate or reason or judge, but simply to see – which involves much more than our eyes and isn't simple at all. Erazim Kohák sets the scene:

> Plato's metaphorical prisoner labours through the stage of *dianoia* or reasoning not in order to construct a hypothesis but to reach the point at which he can see, grasp in a direct awareness, the idea of the Good. Almost three millennia later, it is *seeing* that Husserl and Wittgenstein alike call for in the face of the spiritual crisis of the West: not to speculate but to *see* the sense of it all. Reflection and speculation remain no more than cunningly devised fables if they are not grounded in what, paraphrasing Calvin Schrag, we could call the prephilosophical and prescientific matrix of self-understanding and world-comprehension. Though philosophy must do much else as well, it must, initially, *see* and, thereafter, ground its speculation ever anew in seeing.[11]

'True philosophy entails learning to see the world anew,' says Merleau-Ponty.[12] Still, doesn't thinking – or indeed seeing – in the service of a single cause simply substitute fanatical for fantastical thinking, vis-à-vis Chomsky? This is certainly a real risk, and not one I wish to sidestep. I would counter, however, that while it is not possible to escape the earthly foundations of our thinking and being in the world (which may itself be seen as a totalising fact of life), an attention and attunement to our earthly entanglements is not restrictive but emancipatory; an enrichment compared to the at once deafeningly inundated and steadily sedated sedentary life that many of us have learnt to lead in modern, imperial societies. As

---

9 In Nicholas Allott, Chris Knight & Neil Smith (eds.), *The Responsibility of Intellectuals. Reflections by Noam Chomsky and others after 50 years* (University College London Press, 2019), 104–106. See also Noam Chomsky and Robert Pollin, *Climate Crisis and the Global Green New Deal. The Political Economy of Saving the Planet* (London: Verso, 2020).

10 'Marx says that revolutions are the locomotive of world history. But perhaps it is quite otherwise. Perhaps revolutions are an attempt by the passengers on this train – namely, the human race – to activate the emergency brake.' Quoted in Michael Löwy, *Fire Alarm: Reading Walter Benjamin's 'On the Concept of History'* (London: Verso, 2005), 66–67.

11 Kohák, *The Embers and the Stars*, xxi.

12 Maurice Merleau-Ponty, *Phenomenology of Perception* (New York: Routledge, 2012), lxxxv.

David Abram puts it in *Becoming Animal:* 'I'm embedded in this world, yes – but I am not bound, not imprisoned. There's a new freedom I sense, a looseness, an improvisational openness between myself and the beings around me.'[13] Now, it is this improvisational openness, this looseness, this newfound freedom which is at stake in eco-phenomenology and in my thusly informed take on the task of humanity's responsibility for itself; which, ecologically speaking, equates to our responsibility for all life, past, present, and future.

What Abram is experiencing and voicing is not only the political truism that genuine freedom entails numerous responsibilities – 'no man is an island, entire of itself,' preached English poet John Donne in 1642, or to paraphrase Russian anarchist Mikhail Bakunin from 1867, liberty without solidarity is privilege and injustice, while solidarity without liberty is slavery and despotism – but rather a sense of embodied emancipation that comes from experientially recognising that *I* belong to Earth, that I am *of* the earth, not just before and after life, but *in* life. That my flesh is entwined with the flesh of the world, to use a Merleau-Pontian expression. This is what we might call an ecophenomenological leitmotif, if not *the* leitmotif of the genre: the earth as originary ground (Husserl), as sheltering agent (Heidegger), and as wild being (Merleau-Ponty). In the following, I will briefly trace this theme of the earth regarded as constitutive and caring ground, what most aboriginal cultures have historically identified with a kind, birthing, embracing, in short, mothering being.

3. The Earth, Dead or Alive

In a famous fragment from ca. 1934, known in English as "The Earth Does Not Move," and in the original German as "Umsturz der kopernikanischen Lehre," Husserl writes that, 'Movement occurs on or in the earth, away from it or off it. In the primordial shape of its representations, the earth itself does not move and does not rest; only in relation to it are movement and rest given as having their sense of movement and rest' at all.[14] From the point of view of lived experience, claims Husserl, Earth is not first and foremost the Copernican space-object that it scientifically is, but rather the arch-body that gives rise to movement and rest in the first place. The Earth, or lower case earth, is what environs every aspect of our everyday lives, yet we don't usually – in the natural attitude, that is – see it. Taking

---

13 David Abram, *Becoming Animal: An Earthly Cosmology* (New York: Vintage Books, 2010), 98.
14 Edmund Husserl, "Foundational Investigations of the Phenomenological Origin of the Spatiality of Nature: The Originary Ark, the Earth, Does Not Move," printed in *Husserl at the Limits of Phenomenology* (Evernston: Northwestern University Press, Merleau-Ponty 2002), 118.

a cue from Heidegger's tool analysis (in which he demonstrates how artefacts go unnoticed in our daily dealings with them, until they cease working or we start studying them), so it is with natural entities too, even all the way up, or down if you will, to the biggest terrestrial being there is, Earth itself. Analogously, we recognise earth's prereflective presence as primordial ground – or as David Abram puts it, as 'the forgotten basis of all our awareness'[15] – best by or in its environmental breakdown. In other words, it's not until the earth StAnDs oUt and dramatically and climatically announces itself through floods and fires that we truly notice it. And conversely, perhaps it is for lack of *actually* seeing it, which means acknowledging, respecting and caring for it, that we are ever able to tear the earth asunder in the first place. As Abram asks, 'What is climate change if not a consequence of failing to respect or even to notice the elemental medium in which we're immersed? Is not global warming, or global weirding, a simple consequence of taking the air for granted?'[16] He elaborates:

> We don't speak of the air between our body and a nearby tree, but rather the empty space between us. It's empty. Just an absence of stuff, without feeling or meaning. A void. / And hence, a perfect place to throw whatever we hope to a-void. The perfect dump site for the unwanted byproducts of our industries, for the noxious brew of chemicals exhaled from the stacks of our factories and power plants and refineries, and the stinging exhaust belching forth from our fossil-fueled vehicles – spewing from automobiles and airplanes, cruise ships and tug boats and giant tankers lugging thick tar sands oil to be processed in foreign ports. Even the most opaque, acrid smoke billowing out of the pipes will dissipate and disperse, always and ultimately dissolving into the invisible. It's gone. Out of sight, out of mind.[17]

'Just an absence of stuff, without feeling or meaning [and so] a perfect place to throw whatever we hope to a-void.' The same may be said of oceans and lands, rivers and forests, and ultimately, of the entire planet. Even if injuries sustained by surface milieus are more tangible and visible than exhaust emissions literally vanishing into thin air, they basically suffer from the same kind of neglect. They too go unnoticed, only, what afflicts them is not so much a failure to directly see them and their destruction (though the cover-up and turning-a-blind-eye business is obviously booming, so it is that too), but rather a structural and cultural failure to recognise and respect their being as living and loveable to begin with. But there's more going on here than neglect or omission, I postulate, for it takes more to kill a planet than not paying attention. Even though the so-called negative inattention is an important component of deadseeing, the preservation of an

---

15 David Abram, *The Spell of the Sensuous. Perception and Language in a More-Than-Human World* (New York: Vintage Books, 2017[1996]), 44.
16 David Abram, "The Commonwealth of Breath" in *Atmospheres of Breathing*, eds. Lenart Škof & Petri Berndtson (New York: SUNY Press, 2018), 263.
17 Abram, "The Commonwealth of Breath", 264.

equally deadening and deadened posture-cum-culture requires coordinated and sustained efforts as well.

When we emit greenhouse gasses into the atmosphere, we don't actually see the damage. That's not the case when we clear-cut forests or pollute waterways. Those actions leave behind palpable scars on the land, and on communities that live on it, so in those cases we must do more than passively let it pass and not recognise its impacts. Instead, we must actively convince each other and ourselves that, while they (say, rivers and forests) may not be a void like the global dump in the sky above and around us, they are – which is to say, again, that we have rendered them such – void of feelings and interests, not to mention intelligence. This is the power and purpose of Westernism, A Worldview Inc., which somewhat paradoxically "animates" capitalism and legitimises resourcism. Why paradoxical? Because capitalism itself is only kept alive by this sustained campaign of death in both the literal and a public relations sense: by actually killing the planet – poisoning it, exhausting it, erasing it, etc. – all the while convincing us that it was "in fact" never alive and therefore cannot be killed, *not really.* Like the air that we "naturally" or "normally" see as empty rather than satiated with life-giving oxygen – and whoever has struggled for air at altitude, underwater, or in outer space will appreciate the difference – we have construed and come to view reality *in toto* as completely void of properties that make it worthy of our appreciation save for whatever material, instrumental or economic *abstract* value we have decided it holds for us. It's not that we are sawing off the branch we're sitting on. It's that we have somehow agreed that the tree of life is no tree at all, or if it is, that trees are evidently worth more dead than alive. In the 1799 words of William Blake: 'The tree which moves some to tears of joy is in the eyes of others only a green thing which stands in the way.' Confronted with worlds of natural wonder, we no longer see holy creation or awesome symbioses. Instead, we are simply, obsessively, looking to make a killing.

Well, not you and I of course. *We* don't. So then who exactly is this carefree, wicked we?

The problem of 'the we' is a tainted one in climate justice discussions, and it merits much more serious consideration than this digression allows. Suffice it to say that this majority-we likely refers to humanity *and* capitalism *and* rich countries *and* middle-class white folks, and whomever else we, the minority-we, want to include for derision. I hope, if it isn't clear already, that by the end of this text you will see why I think these distinctions – including the Anthropocene versus Capitalocene debate that follows from them – aren't of the essence, which is not the same as discounting them altogether. The short of it is simply that no human being alive today can escape the universal force field of deadseeing; it is everywhere, whether we mindlessly reproduce it or actively fight against it, or a bit of both, in any case, its presence is nonetheless absolute, or something very near it.

4. Freedom from the Earth

Here we will return to the phenomenological theme of the earth-ground (the *sol* in solastalgia). In "The Origin of the Work of Art," Heidegger writes of 'that on which and in which man bases his dwelling. We call this ground the *earth*. What this word says,' Heidegger elaborates, 'is not to be associated with the idea of a mass of matter deposited somewhere, or with the merely astronomical idea of a planet. Earth is that whence the arising brings back and shelters everything that arises without violation. In the things that arise, earth is present as the sheltering agent.'[18] The first thing we notice is how Heidegger corroborates Husserl's anti-Copernican revolution (*Umsturz*), agreeing that earth, phenomenologically speaking, is not *primarily* what astronomers and other scientists hold, but rather 'that whence the arising brings back and shelters everything that arises without violation.' What exactly does this mean though? In short, Heidegger's interpretation adds an ethical dimension to Husserl's initial reconfiguration, so, moving from human beings being a part of the biosphere, intertwined in the flesh of the world, we now have the earth-ground playing an active role as sheltering agent. Not only is humanity in a reciprocal and inevitable relationship with the earth (cf. the etymologies of human from *humus*, earth, and Hebrew *adam*, man, from *adamah*, ground), but more importantly, this is not a neutral fact. It comes with a whole host of ethical implications and commitments, just like any relation of kin or kith does, and moreover, it highlights the fundamental inseparability of ethics and metaphysics that is at the heart of all ecophenomenologically minded philosophy; that the earth moulds people no less than they alter it, and that our catastrophic behaviour towards the planet stems, ultimately, from our confusion that we are somehow separate from it; and from our failure, which is related, to grasp the earth-ground that shelters us as a living, breathing and kindred being. But also, that if we let it, this philosophical reconfiguration has the potential to bring us back down to earth, and make us see, with Heidegger, that freedom is not 'a property of man,' and that we should rather consider human being 'a possibility of freedom'.[19] We do not, as it were, have freedom. *It is freedom that has us.*

But if freedom has us, how is that freedom at all? Isn't having synonymous with owning, and if we do not fully own ourselves, mustn't we then concede to some kind of determinism? This is merely my native-European mind freewheeling, *reasoning*. Let us take an example of Abram's that I hinted at earlier. Husserl and Heidegger both apply the preposition *in* as well as *on* when referencing the earth, no doubt to underscore the more unusual use (to modern ears at least) of the two:

---

18 Martin Heidegger, *Poetry, Language, Thought* (New York: HarperCollins, 2001), 41.
19 Martin Heidegger, *The Essence of Human Freedom. An Introduction to Philosophy* (London & New York: Continuum, 2002), 93.

'Movement occurs on or in the earth...' writes Husserl, while for Heidegger the earth is 'that on which and in which man bases his dwelling.' Their prepositional awareness lines up nicely, then, with Abram's later assertion that we live 'immersed *in the depths* of this breathing planet' (see below), and this so-called elemental situatedness is, I will submit, instructive also for understanding what it means to be (an expression of) a possibility of freedom (Heidegger), and how that might lead to a new sense (feeling and meaning) of freedom (Abram).

Like relearning to see the air as something rather than nothing, as meaning-full rather than a void – or perhaps *from* relearning to see the eairth thusly – we might also begin to see and re-cognise freedom as an element to swim or soar in, and indeed to drown or crash in. And if we succeed in so readjusting our eyes and minds and hearts, we might finally see, i.e. real-ize, that our freedom is not, properly understood, ours. That we are but *administrators of freedom*, as Heidegger puts it,[20] and that "our" freedom, to the extent that we get to instantiate our freedom-potentiality, relies entirely on our affinity to the earth, which I call *earthlinity* – a major part of which is how we view and narrate (including orate) and otherwise negotiate that relationship. Here is Abram's passage in full:

> The air is not a random bunch of gases simply drawn to earth by the earth's gravity, but an elixir generated by the soils, the oceans, and the numberless organisms that inhabit this world, each creature exchanging certain ingredients for others as it inhales and exhales, drinking the sunlight with our leaves or filtering the water with our gills, all of us contributing to the composition of this phantasmagoric brew, circulating it steadily between us and nourishing ourselves on its magic, generating ourselves from its substance. It is as endemic to the earth as the sandstone beneath my boots. Perhaps we should add the letter *i* to our planet's name, and call it "Eairth," in order to remind ourselves that the "air" is entirely a part of the eairth, and the *i*, the I or self, is wholly immersed in that fluid element.
>
> The gilt-edged clouds overhead are not plunging westward as the planet rolls beneath them because they themselves are a part of the rolling Eairth. Creatures of the embracing air, of an invisible but nonetheless material layer of this planet, the clouds accompany the Eairth as it turns, their shapeshifting bodies drifting this way and that with the winds. And we, imbibing and strolling through that same air, do not then live on the eairth but *in* it. We are enfolded within it, permeated, carnally immersed *in the depths* of this breathing planet.[21]

Like the ocean of air-awareness that engulfs and sustains us, '*freedom must itself, in its essence*,' says Heidegger, '*be more primordial than man*' (his italics).[22] Heidegger doesn't exactly specify how freedom comes about, or how it is, i.e. its ontology. Instead, though, we get elaborate arguments for freedom's grounding

---

20 Heidegger, *The Essence of Human Freedom*, 93.
21 David Abram, *Becoming Animal*, 101.
22 Heidegger, *The Essence of Human Freedom*, 93.

in organic existence – itself a version of the problem of mind-life continuity – from subsequent phenomenologists of the ecological "persuasion," principally Hans Jonas' *The Phenomenon of Life* from 1966, but also from the closing chapter of Merleau-Ponty's *Phenomenology of Perception*, 1945. These are entirely too broad avenues to pursue in this essay, but they are important wayfinding markers to be aware of as we venture on. My point here is to suggest that freedom too, as a way of explaining Heidegger's conception of primordial freedom, might be seen as – indeed, that it is – a phantasmagoric brew, an elixir concocted by the totality of earth's myriad collaborators in life, like the air in Abram's quote above. Which is to say that human freedom is not a cloak that we don and ditch at will, but rather the very skin we are born into, the flesh that bears us. As Merleau-Ponty writes in his aforementioned chapter on freedom, 'To be born is to be simultaneously born of the world and to be born into the world. The world is always already constituted, but also never completely constituted [...] there is never determinism and never an absolute choice.'[23] We are inevitably free *and* unfree. 'We choose our world and the world chooses us,' so 'freedom is always an encounter between the exterior and the interior,' which is why he, Merleau-Ponty, follows Husserl in talking about a 'field of freedom' and 'conditioned freedom,' with 'immediate possibilities and more distant possibilities.'[24] As Merleau-Ponty shows us, freedom is something we do (the 'we' is left open-ended for now, but ecophenomenology suggests all living creatures aka earthlings partake in some form of free activity), yet at the same time '*your* freedom cannot will itself without emerging from its singularity and without willing freedom *in general.*'[25] In short, my freedom, in the form of commitments, both contributes to and draws on the atmospheric elixir (Abram's wording) of general freedom which emanates from all living beings, all of us beneficiaries of and co-creators in freedom.

5. Atmospheres of Inhumanity

The statements above are, of course, metaphysical, and should not obscure the fact that people can and do violate other people's freedoms all the time. Flesh is chained and skin can be cut, and yet, freedom itself is elemental. Which leaves the greatest (cosmic) implication for last, i.e. for now: that freedom exists, *that it can only exist,* on Earth. Freedom is a function of this blue planet, a dimension of our biospheric being and belonging, of our e-co-existence which constitutes the holy fountain of all personal, earthly freedoms (holy in the pre-Christian sense of

---

23 Merleau-Ponty, *Phenomenology*, 480.
24 Merleau-Ponty, *Phenomenology*, 481.
25 Merleau-Ponty, *Phenomenology*, 483.

'that [which] must be preserved whole or intact, that cannot be transgressed or violated'[26]), because only from *it* may *I* begin to aspire for the heavens at all. Earth is inextricable, then, in this grounding sense, from Heidegger's interpretation of freedom as 'the ground of the possibility of existence, the root of being and time,'[27] and the kicker is of course that once we learn to appreciate our own earthlinity, we no longer need or want to escape and transcend this bond – to be free to do, as it were, whatever we please. To illustrate this point, here is Native American scholar Jack D. Forbes on the total worldview of Native peoples and their relation to religion, the practise and the word:

> The life of Native American peoples revolves around the concept of the sacredness, beauty, power and relatedness of all forms of existence. In short, the ethics or moral values of Native people are part and parcel of their cosmology or total world view. Most Native languages have no word for "religion" and it may be true that a word for religion is never needed until a people no longer have it. As Ohiyesa (Charles Eastman) said: "Every act of his [the Indian's] life is, in a very real sense, a religious act."
> Religion is, in reality, living. Our religion is not what we profess, or what we say, or what we proclaim; our religion is what we do, what we desire, what we seek, what we dream about, what we fantasize, what we think – all of these things – twenty-four hours a day. One's religion, then, is one's life, not merely the ideal life but the life as it is actually lived.[28]

All these names for 'religion,' 'spirituality,' 'ethics,' 'freedom,' 'justice,' etc.... apart from what we (think we) know them to mean, does their very existence in language, perhaps their abstraction into language in the first place, tell us more? Are they also the result of some original loss, or fall, or sin? It's at least possible, I think, that the separation and development of these human affairs of the heart, for lack of a better term, into specialised spheres of human existence has meant, or signals, that they have each lost touch – to what degree we can debate – with reality in terms 'not merely [of] the ideal life but the life as it is actually lived,' i. e. the lifeworld. Which reminds me of Marx's thesis that philosophers have so far only understood the world but should strive to change it; that ethics must be embodied, theory anchored in practice, learning in living. Or with a contemporary example from German sociologist Hartmut Rosa who writes here of justice as an abstract (modern, male) principle as opposed to something that naturally (motherly, kindly) *lives in* and *grows from* a person, or rather from a person's relationship to the world in both spatial and temporal terms; *horizontally*, from

---

26 See *Online Etymology Dictionary*, https://www.etymonline.com/word/holy#etymonline_v_12110.
27 Heidegger, *The Essence of Human Freedom*, 93.
28 Jack D. Forbes, *Columbus and Other Cannibals. The Wétiko Disease of Exploitation, Imperialism and Terrorism* (New York: Seven Stories Press, 2008, revised edition, orig. 1979), 15, his italics and addendum.

one's connection to the current of history, including future generations, and *vertically*, e.g. to nature, as that which we in the present share with, and care for on behalf of, our children both actual and metaphorical, i.e. our descendants:

> A person who feels himself cut off in his existence from past and future generations has little reason to allow himself to be influenced by such abstract principles of justice while a person who feels the *current of history* flowing through her, who feels such a responsive connection to her ancestors and descendants that they *concern* her in some way, has no need of such principles to justify living sustainably; she experiences material restrictions not as restrictions at all, but as an element of the establishment of resonance and thus of a successful life.[29]

Forbes' entire 1979 book, *Columbus and Other Cannibals*, is a kindred way of understanding the deadening'n'deadened attitudinal matrix that I call deadseeing. In very broad brushstrokes, Forbes asserts that Columbus and the cult of holocaustic colonialists that he fronted did not do what they did, and we, their heirs, do not do what we do today, purely or primarily out of greed or because of misguided ethics, but rather because they were, and we are, '*mentally ill or insane, the carrier[s] of a terribly contagious psychological disease, the* wétiko *psychosis.*'[30] Forbes' idea is very similar then to that of Paul Shepard in his 1982 book entitled *Nature and Madness*. Like Forbes, Shepard also blames our species' ceaseless despoiling of the earth on a mass psychopathology – his focus is pedagogical as it concerns the failed development of self, of ontogenesis or ontogeny, rather than colonial, imperial and settler sentiments – but because Shepard didn't name this madness aka immaturity, I stick with Forbes' term. '*Wétiko* is a Cree term,' Forbes writes, 'which refers to a cannibal or, more specifically, to an evil person or spirit who terrorizes other creatures by means of terrible evil acts, including cannibalism. [...] I have come to the conclusion that *imperialism and exploitation are forms of cannibalism* [... which], as I define it, *is the consuming of another's life for one's own private purpose or profit.*'[31] What is the connection between this psychopathology, the wétiko psychosis, and deadseeing? If a mass psychological dis-ease afflicts much or most of humanity today, and if it is what is fundamentally leading us down a collective path of self-imposed ecocide and suicide, then the "treatment" we need and must seek out is therapeutic. If, on the other hand, the "diagnosis" is philosophical, that is, *phenomenological*, then the "cure" is, with a deliberately unflattering term, more superficial. Put differently, if the problem is in the eyes – widely considered, including the eyes of the skin, to use Juhani Pallasmaa's poetic phrase – rather

---

29 Hartmut Rosa, *Resonance. A Sociology of Our Relationship to the World* (Cambridge: Polity Press, 2019), 428.
30 Forbes *Columbus*, 22, his italics.
31 Forbes *Columbus*. 24, his italics.

than the mind or in the brain, then its resolution also lies in this medial, peripheral land: in the eyes, the skin, the middle ground where outer meets inner, in the vision rather than the wiring. Which is not to suggest that Forbes' and Shepard's focus on psychopathology is misguided, for the way we perceive the world (lit: take it in, grasp it) inevitably shapes our minds just as much as our minds (in)form our perceptions. It is only a matter of where to set in first; of where to begin to unlearn, and thus unravel, this crisis-of-seeing/crisis-of-mind matrix. And moreover, if the mind or spirit is outside as much as inside us (as this traditional, cyclical thinking holds[32]) then such psychopathology, whether in the form of a worldwide wétiko psychosis or a collective immaturity, is worldly as much as it is mental, pneumatic as much as it is personal. It is, in short, *atmospheric.*

'Just as nature penetrates to the center of my personal life and intertwines with it,' writes Merleau-Ponty, 'behaviors also descend into nature and are deposited there in the form of a cultural world.' Just as we live with/in the earthly elements of soil, air, and water, so, too, we live with/in worlds of our own making; worlds which each 'emits an atmosphere of humanity.'[33] Our behaviour and actions literally go into nature and change it. They are sedimented there, to use another Merleau-Pontian expression, and as climate change makes all-too clear, what's stored in nature can easily come back to haunt us. Now it is from with/in this grounding of behaviour deposited in nature that we begin to see how our actions, guided as they are by our *visions* of the world, ultimately form the world we live in. If we see a dead world, we project a dead world, and so make a dead world. A dead rose is a dead rose is a dead rose; say it long enough, see it long enough, and it is so.

But deadseeing is a two-edged sword: it taints the deadseer's own being just as much as it paints the world (imperial grey, monochrome, b/w). It's internally affective just as much as it is externally effective. In advertisement tongue, what you see is what you get, a dead world. But you also are what you eat, meaning, you become what you take in. And if you see and project a dead world, you end up deadened too, just another machine in a mechanistic world. In that sense we really are killing the planet out of habit. Belief and perception really can and do change the world, but broadly speaking – say, over the last centuries – it hasn't been for the better. In the words of radical sociologist John Holloway, *we are the*

---

[32] 'Is consciousness really the special possession of our species? Or is it, rather, a property of the breathing biosphere – a quality in which we, along with the woodpeckers and the spreading weeds, all participate? Perhaps the apparent "interiority" we ascribe to the mind has less to do with a separate consciousness located somewhere *inside me* and another entirely separate and distinct consciousness that sits *inside you*, and more to do with the intuition that we are both situated *within it* – a recognition that we are carnally immersed in an awareness that is not, properly speaking, ours, but is rather the earth's' (Abram, "The Commonwealth of Breath," 265).

[33] Merleau-Ponty, *Phenomenology*, 363.

crisis of capitalism.[34] This is what it means to be indigenous not to a place but to a way of life, and in our case – presuming you are more or less like me – one that is killing the planet. We are living our joint destruction as if a parasitic organism was controlling our minds and bodies via our eyes and brains, terraforming our habitats through our habits. Now, 'The question, of course, is: if we humans are the cause, can we change ourselves enough to change our impacts?'[35]

6. The Imperial Mode of Living and Dying

Finally, a third conceptual framework related to what I call deadseeing, and Forbes called a cannibalistic mass psychosis, is Ulrich Brand and Markus Wissen's concept of the imperial mode of living, which in their words is

> … a group of problems that have so far made an emancipatory, socio-ecological transformation more difficult [...] It is deeply imbedded in political institutions, the economy, culture and mentalities; in the ways in which people see themselves in the world; in the interests of relevant political and social actors; and in the practises of everyday life [...] The core idea of the concept is that everyday life in the capitalist centres is essentially made possible by shaping social relations and society-nature relations *elsewhere*, i.e. by means of (in principle) unlimited access to labour power, natural resources and [so-called] sinks [e.g. rainforests and oceans]…[36]

In short, what Brand and Wissen's concept emphasises is the externalisation of both costs and consequences. As such, their book belongs to a current trend in leftist social theory – especially that of the heartland of European empire, i.e. Germany – to take up again concepts such as the lifeworld (Husserl), everyday life (Lefebvre), and forms of life (Adorno). Another example would be Stephan Lessenich's 2019 book *Living Well at Others' Expense*. Now what is externalisation if not, in Forbes' terms, the consumption of another's life? Or, more precisely: it is the orchestrated consumption of many others' lives, both for one's own instant gratification, in the form of iPhones and Pop-Tarts, SoMe likes and sugar highs, but always also – systemically, symbolically, even ritualistically – for all of ours collective sustained satisfaction; a secular transubstantiation of millions of mundane meals that ultimately preserve the imperial *corpus politicum*, and with it,

---

34 John Holloway, *We Are the Crisis of Capitalism. A John Holloway Reader* (Oakland: PM Press). Also see, e.g., David Wood, *Reoccupy Earth. Notes Toward an Other Beginning* (New York: Fordham University Press, 2019), or Frédéric Lordon, *Willing Slaves of Capital. Spinoza and Marx on Desire* (London: Verso, 2014).

35 Deborah Bird Rose, *Wild Dog Dreaming. Love and Extinction* (University of Virginia Press, 2011), 2.

36 Ulrich Brand & Markus Wissen, *The Imperial Mode of Living. Everyday Life and the Ecological Crisis of Capitalism* (London: Verso, 2021), 39–40.

our "sacred" forms of "better" living. Certainly, the consumptive act itself needn't be satisfying to any one person. In fact it seldom is. Most of the time most of us are simply blind to it, and that is indeed a key function of deadseeing,[37] which we'll now call *the perceptual mode of the mode of imperial living*; the phenomenological and ideological component that lives inside as well as outside us; the imperial wind-mind that permeates and impregnates all, whispering sweet dreams of progress and prosperity in our ears.

From within the imperial mode of living, plain old eating can only be satisfied via the intricate networks of, and on the backs of, other people's lives; what Brand and Wissen call the elsewhere(s). The word 'satisfaction' offers us a clue, from *satis* (enough) plus *facere* (make): within capitalist societies, we don't have a choice but to feed (we call it rely) on *extra-imperial* others and elsewheres; our cores simply cannot sustain themselves, and we literally cannot feed ourselves, without the eternal, infernal expropriation of the periphery, i.e., without cannibalising it.[38] Today we generally get our food from fields so depleted of natural nutrients that we have to import potash fertiliser from faraway mines and saturate our soils with synthetic solutions just for it to feed us, and poorly so. Even worse, we, which is to say our industrial agriculture, make absolutely sure that before planting any crops, the soil we think is dead, see as dead, and want to be dead, is in fact dead. So we shoot it up with soil fumigants, junkie style, killing everything organic, before subsidising the crop with ammonium nitrate, a substance otherwise famed for its eerie ability to blow up things. In short, we eat how we perceive. Our actual eating is just one aspect of how we consume the world: like it's dead dirt rather than living soil. And because we eat and treat it that way, it is that way. Ours is an antibiotic way of death instead of a probiotic way of life. Imperial capitalism doesn't know enough. It has no place for it and no use for it. Try as you might, you cannot satiate a zombie.[39]

'It would seem there is an inherent instability to the framework of world-as-resource that impels it to devour what it enflames.'[40] Not only is deadseeing the

---

37 Jacques Derrida writes, 'No one can deny seriously any more, or for very long, that men do all they can in order to dissimulate this cruelty [to animals but it's true of all non-human nature] or to hide it from themselves; in order to organize on a global scale the forgetting or misunderstanding of this violence, which some would compare to the worst cases of genocide (there are also animal genocides: the number of species endangered because of man takes one's breath away).' *The Animal That Therefore I Am* (New York: Fordham University Press, 2008), 25–26.
38 Also see Nancy Fraser, *Cannibal Capitalism. How our System is Devouring Democracy, Care, and the Planet – and What We Can Do About it* (London: Verso Books 2022).
39 For more on the relationship between perception, ideology and worldview vis-à-vis land use, earthcare and agriculture, see Vandana Shiva, *Monocultures of the Mind. Perspectives on Biodiversity and Biotechnology* (Zed Books, 1993), and George Monbiot, *Regenesis. Feeding the World without Devouring the Planet* (Penguin Books Ltd, 2022).
40 Amitav Gosh, *The Nutmeg's Curse. Parables for a Planet in Crisis* (John Murray, 2021), 73.

default perceptual mode of modernity, as in, it is the standard mode; the Empire of deadseeing is default in a second sense too: defunct, derelict, dead. When the system runs out of elsewheres to devour, it doesn't cease consuming but instead turns autosarcophagic; it eats itself, like the accursed Greek prince Erysichthon. But that is the literal definition of unsustainability, and so it cannot last. Which is why this civilisation *is already dead*, to use Rupert Read's framing: either it dies of its own devices – and a horrid death of simultaneous collapses of economies, ecosystems and ultimately societies that will be – or it transforms itself to such a degree that it will no longer be itself. Either way, this civilisation is finished.[41] To use a fitting term from extinction studies, it is 'functionally dead'. Or another term of no less chilling origins, it is in 'walking ghost phase' (an initial period of apparent health after a fatal radiation poisoning). And still acolytes of the deadseeing status quo insist that it is simply in man's nature (I use the gendered term deliberately) to reach for the stars, to want more, to strive. So you might burn your wings from time to time, but that's innovation baby. And frankly, they say, it's bravery.

The doubly default *predatory mode* of deadseeing promotes an entrepreneurial worldview in which competition trumps cooperation, where economic growth is both measure and end, and where strength is understood as the power to amass. If a fateful hunger to some degree lives in the entrails of us all, it is kept alive by the consumption of our eyes as we perceive and process the world every day, in and out, over and over. But is there really no other way to take in the world? A way that feels less like a land grab, and more like an act of love?

Indigenous scholar Viola Cordova recounts a story of ancestral human-bird communion that her grandmother's grandfather, Viola's great-great-grandfather, would tell: 'Once, a long time ago, the People were hungry. [Then] In the midst of this despair, Ravens began to appear among the People.' These birds would, over days and weeks, try to lead the People to food. But the People could not or would not understand. So the People trap a Raven and interrogate him. But the bird cannot talk in chains. Only when they free the bird does he speak and lead them to his land where food is plenty. The People see that the birds were trying to help them all along, and so, give prayers of thanksgiving to the birds. Finally, about to journey home, a bird larger than any the People have ever seen before bids them farewell: 'There will come a time, said Old Raven, when our peoples will not speak directly to one another. We will have different languages, different homes, but we will always experience hunger. That is the way of beings on this

---

41 Rupert Read & Samuel Alexander, *This Civilisation is Finished. Conversations on the end of Empire, and what lies beyond* (Melbourne: Simplicity Institute, 2019).

Earth. The next time our children come among you, he said, do not ignore them. They come to invite you to a feast.'[42]

Were the blackbirds of my own childhood trying to tell *me* something? I don't think it works that way. Probably the birds of Europe gave up talking to human beings a long time ago, when we would only talk to ourselves anyways. Perhaps it is the landscape that speaks, and not so much the beings that belong to it? In any case, I would only want to say that the living landscape and the living earth *is not dead*; and if it no longer speaks to us, directly or indirectly, it is because we have rendered it mute, and ourselves incapable of listening.

Which sounds hopeless, but needn't be.

The absolute numbers of people who see the planet as alive and loveable, i. e. Planeteers, is actually substantial. Yet they remain relatively minor because and as the default mode of deadseeing annexes ever greater swathes of the collective human body and psyche, either as a fully realised way of life – which is properly speaking many ways of death – or as the edenic promised land of prosperity that we are all universally, from the wealthiest to the most wretched of the earth (cf. Frantz Fanon), driven to desire and aspire to. In his appeal for "A Vitalist Politics," Amitav Ghosh writes of the 'countercurrents that have continued to flow around the planet, like a subterranean river, throughout the time in which the mechanistic metaphysic was rising to dominance. […] These were all revolts against the project of reducing the Earth to a clockwork mechanism in which every kind of being was brutishly mute, except for European elites and Euro-descended colonists.'[43] Ghosh's full book is in fact a comprehensive account of the colonial heritage inherent in the concept of deadseeing, not unlike Fanon's book but for the age of ecocide and climate collapse. Or take Aldo Leopold's assertion that opens *A Sand County Almanac:* 'There are some who can live without wild things, and some who cannot. […] Now we face the question whether a still higher 'standard of living' is worth its cost in things natural, wild, and free. For us of the minority [henceforth known as Planeteers, lovers of the land in Leopoldian land-ethical terms], the opportunity to see geese is more important than television, and the chance to find a pasque-flower is a right as inalienable as free speech.'[44] As the saying goes, the revolution will not be televised. Instead it beckons *real intimacy:* an actual, natural involvement with the living reality we are part of.[45] As is, though, the doubly default mode of deadseeing makes for an

---

[42] Viola Cordova, *How It Is: The Native American Philosophy of V. F. Cordova* (University of Arizona Press, 2007), 11, 13.
[43] Ghosh 2021, 235.
[44] Aldo Leopold, *A Sand County Almanac. And Sketches Here and There* (Oxford UP, 1987), vii.
[45] See for example: (1) Rachel Carson, "Help your child to wonder," in *Woman's Home Companion* (July 1956). Published posthumously as *The Sense of Wonder*, Harper and Row 1965. (2) Robert Michael Pyle, "Nature matrix: reconnecting people and nature," in *Oryx* 37:2

almost invisible, seemingly invincible universal blockade against even the tiniest efforts at interspecies intimacy/empathy, let alone to any systemic revolt against the imperial mode of living and dying, with its resourcism, economism, managerialism and entrepreneurialism beaming reverently from billions of desensitised eyes, like the scorching-red laser beams of some retro eco-supervillain.

7. From Deadseeing to Ways of Loving

Etymologically, the adjective 'free' is presumed to derive from the Proto-Indo-European (PIE) root *prī*, meaning 'to love.' Freedom, in the sense of being free to direct one's own life and fate, is claimed therefore to derive from 'beloved' or 'friend,' designating free members of a community or clan, as opposed to those who are unfree, slaves. The *Online Etymology Dictionary* provides further support for this association between freedom and love:

> It is the hypothetical source of/evidence for its existence is provided by: Sanskrit *priyah* "own, dear, beloved," *priyate* "loves;" Old Church Slavonic *prijati* "to help," *prijatelji* "friend;" Welsh *rhydd* "free;" Old English *freo* "exempt from; not in bondage, acting of one's own will," Gothic *frijon* "to love," Old English *freod* "affection, friendship, peace," *friga* "love," *friðu* "peace," Old Norse *Frigg*, name of the wife of Odin, literally "beloved" or "loving."[46]

With Heidegger we saw/said that the earth does not merely or simply *ex-ist* as a static background. Instead it takes an active role, it *in-sists*, in sheltering us, and, I added, in moulding us (and not only in birth but throughout life). Building on Heidegger's elemental reappraisal of freedom, considering it 'the ground of the possibility of existence, the root of being and time,' rather than the 'property of man,' we were able to equate freedom, in this grounding sense, with earth in the tenor of Husserl and Heidegger. Now, as we venture a step further, and see/say that freedom requires, or is born *together with*, love, which is again rooted in kinship, it is possible to truly see – as in, appreciate – the natural and circular, i. e. ecological, affinities that I claim also bind together love and the earth.

What unites (a) the animate earth to which I belong but am not bound, (b) the new sense of freedom I feel following this realisation (Abram 2018), and (c) love? Like Abram, who suggests that we do not live on Eairth but in it; and like Heidegger, who said that freedom does not come from us, but rather we emerge out of it; we may now offer a third conceptual revaluation modelled on the same

---

(2003), 206–214. Reprinted in *Nature Matrix. New and Selected Essays*, (Counterpoint 2020) And (3) Kym Maclaren, "Intimacy as Transgression and the Problem of Freedom," in *Puncta: Journal of Critical Phenomenology* (inaugural issue, 2018), 18–40.

46 See *Online Etymology Dictionary,* https://www.etymonline.com/search?q=freedom.

reversal, namely, that love is not in fact something we possess, that we give and take, but something we are always already *given over to*, immersed and imbedded in, permeated and charged by. Again, I do not mean to suggest that love is universal in the religious sense, or that it is infrangible. The grace of God is clearly inconstant, and the prospect of peace on earth leaves much to be desired.

The point I am making is that the living planet that embraces and sustains us is indistinguishable from the biospheric potentiality from whence we gain 'our' freedom, albeit unequally so, as well as from the medium from whence we draw, or do not draw, love. Yes, we owe the world to those who love us and let us love them. But the existence of love itself, that we owe to the living planet, to life on earth; not to Earth the space-rock, but to the earth-ground that is the source of all love and all freedom, that gives us life and every good thing that can come of it: wisdom, justice, peace, fun in the park, football in the street, and so on. Once we see – which is to say, once we *feel* it – that the earth cares for us, it might not seem like a far-out thing of the past to give thanks to the earth, and hopefully to fall (or dive) back *in love* with it. Which, I'll be the first to admit, has the distinct air of stale cliché all over it, but I don't really see a workaround to this problem, other than heroically, and only half-jokingly, declaring myself in the service (not business!) of philosophically substantiating platitudes.

According to the Amerindian Mbyá people, the Universe was born in love.[47] This is a cosmo-metaphysical and possibly metaphorical claim which there is no way to prove or disprove, nor do I think there is any good reason to. What I do however believe we can say with a considerable degree of philosophical confidence is that love – at least as we know it – belongs to this blue planet and this arboreal biosphere. But that, to me, is already the greatest benefit of the theory-practice of ecophenomenology: how a mindful return to the earth might help us re-appreciate reality as inherently kind, wonderful and loveable. How it might, for example, help us recognise that love, like freedom, is a function of life and death on this earth. And ultimately, how it might return meaning to our modern lives, not through laborious acts of religious faith or of mechanistic reason, but through embodied efforts to see and love and live anew. Of *being* anew. Of paying attention and tuning into the earth and the elements and everything besides that make up our home planet and our lives with/in it. And then to work to further it through actions of care, connection, compassion and healing in the face of death and suffering and injustice, which is also part of the world we have created and therefore live in, but needn't be the dominant force. Love is, as many a 'love-doctor' has claimed, something we do and make together. As such, to save the planet and ourselves, both literally and morally, we must strive to be and to become, in all that we do, desire and think, Planeteers: pioneers for a new story.

---

47 Forbes, *Columbus*, 6.

Articles

Robert W. Rix
(University of Copenhagen)

The Spectre Barber: Shaving the Ghost in the Eighteenth and Nineteenth Centuries

Abstract

The article discusses the transmission of the folktale at a critical juncture when it moved into the mainstream of polite literature. The case study is Johann Karl August Musäus' "Stumme Liebe", included in *Volksmärchen der Deutschen* (1782–1786), a collection that preceded the Brothers Grimm by nearly three decades. Musäus helped spark an interest in the low form of the folktale by re-packaging oral tradition as elegant and humorous stories palatable to a middle-class readership. However, as "Stumme Liebe" was transmitted in print by others, Musäus' conception of the folktale was challenged, and the story itself was radically changed. The article pays particular attention to the retelling of the story in Britain because the changes it underwent in English translation reveal an important cultural history of folktale reception, not least in regard to the Romantic-period renegotiation of the supernatural.

Keywords

Folktale, Johann Karl August Musäus, supernaturalism, ghost story, print culture

This article examines an episode in the transmission of the folktale, as the genre moved into the mainstream of polite literature in the late eighteenth and early nineteenth centuries. Today, the best-known collection of folktales is the Brothers Grimm's *Kinder- und Hausmärchen* (Children's and household tales) (first edition 1812–1815), stories from which are regularly republished and translated. Predating the Grimm's publication by three decades was Johann Karl August Musäus' collection *Volksmärchen der Deutschen* (Folktales of the Germans), published in five volumes between 1782 and 1786. Among the folk tales Musäus included in the collection is "Richilde", the earliest written version of Snow White that we have. For this article, I have chosen to focus on the tale entitled "Stumme Liebe" (mute love), which is printed in the fourth volume of *Volksmärchen*, as a case study. This story became a popular piece, not least because of the memorable section in which a spectral barber shaves the protagonist, Franz, to complete baldness while Franz in return gives the ghost the same treatment.

"Stumme Liebe" is particularly interesting because it is narrated in a style very different from what we expect a folktale to look like today. Thus, I will begin with an examination of Musäus' satirical and highly interpolative narration. As "Stumme Liebe" was transmitted in print across geographical and linguistic borders, what a written-down version of the folktale should look like became a vexed question. I will pay particular attention to the reception of "Stumme Liebe" in Britain because the British translations and debates reveal an important but little-told cultural history of folktale reception. Here, the contrast between what we may categorize as the 'Romantic' and 'non-Romantic' view of the folktale became a focus for discussions.

Committing an oral tale to print usually freezes it into a relatively fixed shape, but the story of the spectral barber challenges that assumption, as it was received in the new intellectual framework of Romanticism. By following the trajectory of the tale, it is possible to exemplify the divide between a pre-Romantic attempt to refine the folktale for bourgeois consumption and the Romantic ideal of the folktale as original *Volkspoesie* (poetry of the people). I argue that behind this divide is also the history of another intellectual change, which concerns the legitimacy of the supernatural, often prevalent in folktales. The question that the mediators of the folktale struggled with was this: should the supernatural be mitigated (if not policed) before it was passed on to a rationally minded audience, or was it to be celebrated as an alternative to a purely 'utilitarian', i.e. quantitatively calculable, idea of the natural universe?

The Discourse of the Folktale

Johann Karl August Musäus (1735–1787) was professor of Ancient Languages and History at the Wilhelm-Ernst-Gymnasium in Weimar but is best known for his abiding interest in vernacular culture. We know from his relative, August von Kotzebue, that Musäus gathered his materials by speaking to old women at their spinning wheels, collecting their stories, and that he would also pay children in the street to tell tales.[1] Musäus explains in the preface to *Volksmärchen* that the tales are 'all local products that have been propagated for many generations from ancestors to grandchildren and descendants through oral tradition', and that 'they are not melted down nor re-minted as the gold coins that used to appear as a strange mixture of Louis XV's portrait often with the wig or nose of his father's

---

[1] "Kotzebue's Historical Literary and Political Anecdotes", in *The German Novelists: Tales Selected from Ancient and Modern Authors in that Language*, ed. and trans. Thomas Roscoe, 4 vols. (London: Henry Colburn, 1826), 3:11.

father'.² What exactly Musäus means by this is not entirely clear, but the essence seems to be that the tales have not been altered to recommend a moral like Charles Perrault did in his *Histoires ou contes du temps passé, avec des moralités* (Tales and stories of the past with morals) (1697). Nonetheless, Musäus did make changes. It is quite clear that the fourteen stories in *Volksmärchen* are not accurate transcriptions of what Musäus heard. If he did not add morals to the traditional stories he wrote down, he manipulated the narration to express an opinion about the worldview of the folktale. This is what will be discussed in this section.

Volksmärchen was predated by Johann Gottfried Herder's pioneering anthology of *Volkslieder* (1778–1779), but Musäus' approach to sources differs from this in several respects. Whereas Herder's collection was an antiquarian work, in which European ballads were translated roughly as he found them (in print), Musäus was intent on transforming oral folk tradition into a fashionably modern and polite entertainment.³ Occasionally, when Musäus uses assonance and rhyming, his writing conveys the tales' origin in oral delivery, but he also furnishes the narration with novelistic elements. For example, Musäus explains in the preface that he has decided to provide the tales with indications of time and place, even though such designations are nondescript in oral tradition.⁴ "Stumme Liebe" is thus assigned to the 1530s, and the scene is set in the Hanseatic city of Bremen, presumably because this location fits the story of Franz, who is a merchant's son. As has been noted, Musäus adds a *couleur locale* to his description of Bremen, including references to the city's geography.⁵

It is not easy to classify "Stumme Liebe" according to recognized categories. We know from sources that he received the story from his niece Caroline Amalie Gildemeister (née Kotzebue) in some form, but we do not know what her version looked like.⁶ It is thus clear that oral material formed the basis of "Stumme Liebe", and its elements derived from the folktale tradition (*Volksmärchen*). However, Musäus' written version is best seen as a *Kunstmärchen*, i. e. a literary fairy tale. To what extent the literary folktale differs from the oral folktale is not clearly demarcated in criticism. The literary tale may be conceptualized and entirely

---

2   J. K. A. Musäus, *Volksmärchen der Deutschen* (Leipzig: Mayer und Wigand, 1842), 14. My translation.
3   For a study of Musäus' adaptation of folktales, see Malgorzata Kubisiak, *Märchen und Meta-Märchen: Zur Poetik der Volksmärchen der Deutschen von Johann Karl August Musäus* (Fernwald: Litblockin, 2002). For a study of comparative aspects, see also David Blamires, *Telling Tales: The Impact of Germany on English Children's Books 1780–1918* (Cambridge: Open Books Publishing, 2009), 51–61.
4   Musäus, *Volksmärchen*, 14.
5   See Hermann Tardel, "Zum Märchen "Stumme Liebe" von Musäus", *Zeitschrift für Volkskunde* 44 (1934): 213–14.
6   Gustav Brandes, *Aus den Gärten einer alten Hansestadt* (Bremen: Arthur Geist, 1939), 5.

authored by a literary writer who has internalized a number of broad themes from tradition and can repeat them to produce something resembling an oral folktale. Hans Christian Andersen's fairy tales are a good example of this. Or it may be that a literary writer/collector/editor produces a version of an actual oral fairy tale, but transfers it to a written discourse and perhaps embellishes it with literary improvements. Such was the case with the Grimm stories in the later editions of their tales.[7] As Jack Zipes has noted, the clearest distinction between *Volksmärchen* and *Kunstmärchen* is their intended audiences: the former was circulated among the lower orders, whereas the latter was published for a book-buying bourgeoisie.[8] It is Musäus' communication with a middle-class, primarily metropolitan audience that will be the focus below. It would be interesting to trace the folklore motifs discernible in "Stumme Liebe" to its parallels in the Aarne-Thompson-Uther index, but the purpose of this article is to move in the other direction, i.e. to identify references in the text that cannot have been part of the oral material. Musäus' use of studied and superimposed irony appears to increase particularly in the central scene featuring the spectral barber. I will suggest that this is because ghosts were one element of folk-culture that came to be seen as incompatible with modernity and the educated middle classes, for whom Musäus wanted to repurpose the traditional fairy tales as a new mode of literary entertainment. But before this argument is unfolded, an ultrashort summary of what is a rather long story is in order.

The young Franz Melchior squanders the inheritance from his father, who was a successful merchant in Bremen. While living in poverty, he falls in love with the neighbour's daughter, Meta. She reciprocates his attention because of Franz' beautiful lute playing, yet never speaks to him (hence their love is 'mute'). To gather enough wealth to marry Meta, Franz decides to go to Antwerp to collect outstanding debts owed to his late father. On the journey, he has several adventures, the most important event takes place in Rummelsburg Castle on the Westphalian border. At night, Franz is visited by a spectre, who appears in a scarlet coat with a barber's knife. Franz submits to the ghost's razor, not knowing whether it is his hair or his head that he will have to lose. Fortunately, it is only his hair that is shaved off, but this is done so thoroughly that even his eyebrows are shorn. As the ghost is about to leave, Franz senses that something is unfulfilled. He therefore sits the ghost down and gives him the same treatment he himself has just received. Afterwards, the ghost thanks Franz because the curse that has prevented him from finding rest is now broken. While alive, the barber had been a

---

7 For a concise account of the debate, see Renata Schellenberg, "Goethe and *Die Neue Melusine:* A Critical Reinterpretation", in *Melusine's Footprint: Tracing the Legacy of a Medieval Myth*, ed. M. Urban, D. F. Kemmis, and M. R. Elmes (Leiden: Brill, 2017), 305–6.
8 Jack Zipes, *Breaking the Magic Spell: Radical Theories of Folk and Fairy Tales*, rev. edn (Lexington, KY: University Press of Kentucky, 2002), 32.

tool of his master's bizarre humour. Visitors were invited into the castle only to be humiliated; the barber was ordered to shave off all their hair, so they would be laughed at in the nearby village when the master kicked them out of the castle. But one day, a holy man who received this harsh treatment, cursed the barber to wander restlessly in death until the same cruel joke was played on him. Thankful for his release from the curse, the spectral barber gives Franz instructions for how to find a hidden treasure chest. Franz locates the promised wealth of buried gold coins and subsequently returns to Bremen to marry Meta as a rich man.

From this summary, one may recognize the hallmarks of a folktale. But when one reads the tale in *Volksmärchen*, it is obvious that Musäus adopts a narrative voice that is lodged in the world of literary discourse. Musäus often echoes the eighteenth-century comic novel by offering intrusive commentary delivered with a somewhat detached, ironic tone. The narration is most intensely intrusive in the ghost section where the omniscient narrator intervenes with snippets of cosmopolitan knowledge and references to exotic subjects. We read how

> a tall thin man entered with a black beard, clothed in an old-fashioned dress and with a gloomy expression and a scowl on his brow, which gave him a serious look. A scarlet mantle was thrown over his left shoulder and his hat was high and pointed ... Then he threw off his mantle, opened a bag, which he carried under his arm, took out instruments for shaving and began to sharpen a shining razor on a broad leather strap he wore on his belt.

This could be part of an oral tale. But we are then told that Franz' willingness to oblige the ghost can be compared to that of a vizier who resigns himself to the Caliph ordering execution by silk thread.[9] Later, just as the barber is leaving, Franz sees his own clean-shaven image in the mirror and realizes 'that the barber had turned him into a Chinese pagoda'.[10] There are also erudite jokes interspersed to entertain a learned readership. For example, that Franz' loneliness in the castle makes him hanker after company, which we are told is the reverse of the Swiss philosopher Johann Georg Zimmermann, who was pent up in the city when he wrote his famous treaty on solitude (*Über die Einsamkeit*, 1756).[11] There are even hints at psychological analysis when Franz decides to commit himself to his fate. When he jumps out from the bed sheets, under which he had hidden, it is with such a 'rapid transition from extreme despondency to fiercest determination', which 'happened so naturally' that we need 'a psychological journal to explain the phenomenon'.[12] And when the spectral barber sits down to be shaved himself, he makes 'as strange grimaces as Erasmus's Ape when imitating its

---

9 Musäus, *Volksmärchen*, 480.
10 Musäus, *Volksmärchen*, 481.
11 Musäus, *Volksmärchen*, 478.
12 Musäus, *Volksmärchen*, 481.

master's shaving'.¹³ This is an allusion to Erasmus of Rotterdam's early sixteenth-century collection of adages, in which apes (*simia*) are used to embody the concept of imitation.

Most readers today would recognize that this level of learned commentary is uncharacteristic of the folktale. Yet it was common narrational strategy in the novel, which had become popular reading for the middle-class reading public, and it was to this audience Musäus wanted his five-volume *Volksmärchen* to appeal. So, what we find here is the recovery of an ostensible authentic idiom of folklore mixed in with a 'novelization' of the story. In other words, the folktale is recreated as a comic novel of the late eighteenth century, such as the novels of Henry Fielding or Laurence Sterne. My argument is that Musäus' *Volksmärchen* can be viewed as a product of the 'contact zone' that came into being between two cultures: the culture of the folktale and the eighteenth-century book market for the middle classes.¹⁴ To the extent that the tongue-in-cheek commentary intervenes in the storyworld of the folktale, we are led in the direction of Mikhail Bakhtin's theory of *heteroglossia*. Bakhtin discusses how the 'intentional diversity of speech' within a novel may leave us with different strata of the text that can be played off against one another, making the text multi-voiced.¹⁵ That a previous text is incorporated, through satire, in a new text is what happens in Musäus' debut novel *Grandison der Zweite* (Grandison the second) (1760) (to which Bakhtin refers).¹⁶ The novel is a send-up of Samuel Richardson's *The History of Sir Charles Grandison* (1753), but Musäus lets a new perspective interact with Richardson's text by imitating it stylistically and undercutting it with satire. This creates *heteroglossia* in similar ways to the works of Musäus' contemporaries Theodor Gottlieb von Hippel and Jean Paul, to whom Bakhtin also refers.

Importantly, the running commentary also provides a satiric voice that lightens, if not deflates, the superstition of the scene. If the belief in ghosts was commonplace among the lower orders, Musäus undercuts such belief to make it palatable for a bourgeois public. If the basic storyline of the folktale is preserved (with its marvellous and supernatural happenings), Musäus' introduction of distance-marking irony leaves readers free from any serious involvement with the fantastic and, perhaps, even invites them to gloat at the credulity of the ghost

---

13 Musäus, *Volksmärchen*, 482.
14 The idea of the 'contact zone' has been used in connection with colonial encounters by Mary Louise Pratt. In "Arts of the Contact Zone", *Profession* (1991): 33–40, she discusses how new and unique narratives and artefacts may emerge from such encounters.
15 M. M. Bakhtin, *The Dialogic Imagination: Four Essays* ([1981] Austin, TX: University of Texas Press, 2008), 294.
16 Bakhtin, *Dialogic Imagination*, 6. Musäus' novel was revised as *Der deutsche Grandison* (1781-1782). For a substantial discussion of this text, see John P. Heins, "German Quixotism, or Sentimental Reading", *Eighteenth Century Fiction* 16, no. 3 (2004): 419-50.

story. The jocular interpolations in the ghost scene function as a literary mechanism that sets up a defensive screen towards the irrational beliefs of the past and makes the folktale available for middle-class enjoyment, as the success of the middle class was seen to hinge on its rationalism, its levelheadedness, and its embrace of a modernism that was critical of the superstition of the past.

Musäus expressed some concern about the folktale in the introduction to volume one of *Volksmärchen:* the imagination (*die Phantasie*) belongs to the lower faculties of the soul and yet 'often rules over the mind like a pretty maid over the master of the house'.[17] The metaphor is jocular, but the suggestion that a wayward imagination can wield an illegitimate, seductive power that undermines the authority of reason was nonetheless an important cultural admonition at the time. Probably, the most famous example of a literary attack on enthusiasm (i. e. religious fanaticism or superstition) is Christoph Martin Wieland's 1764 novel *Der Sieg der Natur über der Schwärmerei, oder Die Abenteuer des Don Sylvio von Rosalva* (The victory of nature over enthusiasm, or the adventures of Don Sylvio of Rosalva). The eponymous protagonist, who is reared on a diet of romances and *The Arabian Nights*, becomes so convinced of the marvellous in the stories that he truly believes it is the governing principle of the world. Wieland makes Don Sylvio's *Schwärmerei* a lesson for his contemporaries: one must show moderation in all things, including the choice of reading material. The waywardness of the imagination was also taken up in Musäus' own *Grandison der Zweite*, although not in the connection with fantastical stories as much as with fiction in general. The novel focuses on the avid reader Herr von Neunhorn, who has an unhealthy fascination with Samuel Richardson's novel to the extent that he believes the fictional character Sir Charles Grandison exists in real life, confusing fact with fiction.

Musäus' choice of introducing an ironic distance in the ghost scene can be seen as a response to rising scepticism towards the supernatural in the eighteenth century. Otto von Graben zum Stein's discussions about apparitions in the volumes of *Unterredungen von dem Reiche der Geister* (Conversations from the realm of spirits), first published in 1731, documented the appearances of ghosts around the world. But the work was banned by the Prussian court, and the belief in spirits was vehemently attacked by other German texts published through the 1740s.[18] Opposition to the supernatural was also worked into several literary texts. For example, the publicist of Enlightenment ideas Gotthold Ephraim Lessing wrote the poem "Die Gespenster" (1747) (The ghosts), which mocks some people's proclivity for superstition. For other critical views, Musaüs prob-

---

17 Musäus, *Volksmärchen*, 9.
18 Rory E. Bradley, 'The Enlightening Supernatural: Ghost Stories in Late Eighteenth-Century Germany', PhD thesis, University of North Carolina at Chapel Hill, pp. 40–41.

ably knew Immanuel Kant's work *Träume eines Geistersehers, erläutert durch Träume der Metaphysik* (1766) (*Dreams of a Spirit-Seer, Illustrated by Dreams of Metaphysics*), which was much discussed at the time. Here, Kant applies caustic irony to question the existence of ghosts and those who believe they can talk to them. As Shane McCorristine formulates it in his study of ghost-lore, modernity was made possible from 'the systematic discrediting of credulity as a vulgar attribute'.[19] This was reflected in the way literary genre was received as either culturally positive or corruptive. Johann Adam Bergk, a leading figure of the German Enlightenment, expressed concerns about the dangers of popular reading, not least ghost stories. In his book *Die Kunst, Bücher Zu Lesen* (1799) (The art of reading books), he warns that such texts manipulate the people's 'natural inclination to the marvellous and the supernatural', making the reader of 'ghost novels' accept an enchanted world 'while his reason falls asleep on the pillow of the inexplicable'.[20] Thus, he advocates a series of correct reading practices for middle-class book culture. Musäus also echoes such concerns, but instead of exorcising the fantastic and supernatural, he 'modernizes' it by treating it in the style of the comic novel.

The Folktale in the Romantic Period

Musäus had realized the appeal of the folktale and the imaginative splendour that it possessed for a cultivated reading audience. But the folktale, which Musäus gave a new life in print, was a haunted place. If the folktale introduced a renewal in the system of literary genres, its revival was also a return of the repressed. It reminded an enlightened middle class of the superstition that they had left behind and was now preserved only among the lower orders, a culture seen as separate from the rational, sober, and pious ways of the bourgeois public. Musäus' literary distance markers, which were discussed above, gave way to new winds of Romanticism and its appreciation of folk culture as the real measure of the nation. It should be remembered that the title of Musäus' volumes was explicitly *Volksmärchen der Deutschen*, indicating that he was mining national-cultural heritage. But with the ascendancy of Romantic thinking, the comic treatment of the supernatural was increasingly seen as inauthentic. Instead, value was put on the natural vitality, simplicity, and uncorruptedness of the folk and their imaginative productions. And although not part of the Romantic movement, Jacob and Wil-

---

19 Shane McCorristine, *Spectres of the Self: Thinking about Ghosts and Ghost-Seeing in England 1750–1920* (Cambridge: Cambridge University Press, 2010), 31.
20 Quoted in Stefan Andriopoulos, *Ghostly Apparitions: German Idealism, the Gothic Novel, and Optical Media* (New York: Zone Books, 2013), 108.

helm Grimm approached the folktale in ways that accorded with these principles. This can be seen in *Kinder und Haus-Märchen* (Children's and household tales), first published 1812-1815. For example, the brothers were resolved to provide philologically accurate renditions of the oral versions they collected. In particular, they wanted to distance themselves from Clemens Brentano and Achim von Arnim's collection *Des Knaben Wunderhorn* (1805-1808) (The boy's magic horn), which was a series of often artificial constructions that played fast and loose with sources. In the preface to the first edition of *Kinder und Haus-Märchen*, we are told that 'no incident has been added or embellished and changed, for we would have shied away from expanding tales already so rich in and of themselves with their own analogies and similarities'.[21] This avowed non-interventionist approach made it unique in Germany at the time.

Yet the claims of a faithful rendition were disingenuous. As Jack Zipes notes, the Brothers Grimm incorporated not only stylistic alterations (especially in later versions) but also 'substantial thematic changes' to appeal to the growing middle-class audience.[22] In particular, the Grimms sanitized the tales they recorded to expand the market for their folktale collection. The result was a 'hybrid form of folklore and literature', which transformed oral material, often crude and sexually explicit, into bourgeois polite entertainment.[23] The Grimms' manipulations of the material were only comprehensively exposed by twentieth-century commentators; but for the reader at the time, the written versions came across as faithful versions of the folktales Jacob and Wilhelm took down from their informants.

One factor of the Grimm tales that contributed to the sense of simplicity was that they were *Erzählen ohne Erzähler* (narrative without narrator), as Tom Kindt points out.[24] That is to say, extradiegetic narration is reduced to its absolute minimum. In contrast, a salient feature of Franz' adventures in "Stumme Liebe" is the omniscient narrator's running commentary on the events. It is here useful to home in on narration in relation to how Musäus' tales were evaluated in Britain, as this reveals something about the way Romantic ideas of simplicity made the learned style of *Volksmärchen* superannuated. The first English edition of Musäus was a translation of five stories, which was published anonymously in 1791 under the title *Popular Tales of the Germans*. In the introduction, it is strangely not the learned style that is addressed – rather there is a concern that the folktales

---

21 Jacob Grimm and Wilhelm Grimm, "Preface", translated in *The Original Folk and Fairy Tales of the Brothers Grimm Book*, ed. and trans. Jack Zipes (Princeton University Press, 2014), 9.
22 Jack Zipes, *The Brothers Grimm: From Enchanted Forests to the Modern World*, 2nd edn (New York; Basingstoke: Palgrave 2002), 31.
23 Maria Tartar, *The Hard Facts of the Grimm. Expanded Edition* (Princeton and Oxford: Princeton University Press, 2019), 41.
24 Tom Kindt, "Der *discours* des aufgeklärten Märchens. Märchenerzählen bei Wieland, Musäus und den Grimms", Fabula. Zeitschrift für Erzählforschung 54, no. 1 (2014): 41-51.

(for being folktales) are 'too plain and artless for the intellectual palate of these times'.[25] Three decades later, after Romantic ideas had made an impact, Edgar Taylor published a selection of the Grimm tales under the title *German Popular Stories... From Oral Tradition* (1823), in which he emphasizes it as a positive that the tales were 'obtained for the most part from the mouths of German peasants'.[26] Thus, when Thomas Carlyle, an avid translator of German works, published a new translation of some of the *Volksmärchen* in 1827, he was painfully aware that the tide had changed in favour of the Brothers Grimm's ostensibly pure draught from the well of undefiled tradition undefiled. Carlyle contextualizes Musäus in a historical perspective: he had access to the 'rude traditional fragments' but gave them 'shape and polish', so it was possible to transfer them 'from the hearths of the common people to the parlors of the intellectual and refined'.[27] Clearly, in the post-Grimm reception of folktales, Musäus' overwrought style had become a liability. Thus, Carlyle insists that one may see in Musäus' tales 'traces of poetry and earnest imagination ... discernible in the original fiction', but also concedes that the author treats his sources with 'levity, and kind, skeptical derision'.[28] This frees him from accusations of morally corrupting readers with his stories of marvels and supernatural event. Yet the application of satire to the originality and simplicity of folklore also comes at a cost:

> The primitive tradition often serves him [Musäus] only as a vehicle for interesting description, shrewd, sarcastic speculation, and gay, fanciful pleasantry, extending its allusions over all things past and present now rising into comic humor, now sinking into drollery, often tasteless, strained, or tawdry, but never dull.[29]

Musäus' novelistic remaking of tradition as satire is clearly seen to be at odds with a Romantic aggrandizement of the folktale as an organic outgrowth of the people. Thus, Carlyle informs the reader that he considered adapting Musäus' tales to fit a simpler aesthetics. Yet he eventually decided against it. What Carlyle hopes the reader will appreciate is that the German writer's sharp wit may find 'some favour' among reading audiences, but he will not plead his case.[30] Carlyle is aware that he was peddling a product that was becoming obsolete in the current literary climate.

In the same year as Carlyle's translation appeared, Walter Scott, the most famous novelist of the day, published an essay on the use of the fantastic in

---

25 n.a., *Popular Tales of the Germans*, 2 vols. (London: J. Murray, 1791), 1:xi.
26 Edgar Taylor, 'Preface', in *German Popular Stories from the Kinder und Hausmärchen*, Kinder- und Hausmärchen *Collected by M. M. Grimm, from Oral Tradition* (London: C. Baldwyn, 1823), v–vi.
27 Thomas Carlyle, *German Romance*, 2 vols. (London: Chapman & Hall, 1827), 1:13.
28 Carlyle, *German Romance*, 1:8.
29 Carlyle, *German Romance*, 1:14.
30 Carlyle, *German Romance*, 1:18.

literature, drawing on his vast collection of German books, most of which were of antiquarian or folklore interest.[31] Scott analyzes Musäus' versions of folktales as having two components: 'the ground work of the story and that which is added by the art of the narrator'.[32] As Scott further observes, the German writer 'takes the narration of the common legend' and 'dresses it up after his own fashion', serving up ancient traditions 'like yesterday's cold meat from the larder', which 'by dint of skill and seasoning' is given 'a new relish for the meal of to day'.[33] Knowing the public's taste of the late eighteenth century, Musäus was aware that 'the simplicity of the unadorned popular legend' would 'obstruct' the possibility of making it popular at the time he was writing'.[34]

Both Scott and Carlyle see Musäus' versions as palimpsests, where different layers of the text are discernible. There was thus a storyworld of the original folktale (the basic sequence of events) and then Musäus' overlays of narrative commentary (part of what Russian Formalism identifies as *suyzhet*). But this is most probably too simplistic a view. Musäus likely organized the plot lines, as well as selected and deselected among story elements, in ways that meant that one cannot just remove the stylistic embellishments to reveal an original preceding text. If Carlyle had resigned himself to a faithful English version, which he gave the title "Dumb Love", others before him attempted to isolate the hypothetical 'original' tale underneath the satirical overlays. In the following, versions published prior to Carlyle's 1827 translation will be discussed in terms of how they sought to extrapolate from the stories a unique insight into the supernatural ideas of the folk.

The Ghost Story: Romantic-Period Translations

The Brothers Grimm only have few ghosts in their tales (the story of "The Stolen Farthings" is the best-known example), but the collection *Gespensterbuch* (Ghost book) (seven volumes 1810–1815), edited by August Apel and Friedrich Laun (pseudonym for Friedrich August Schulze), filled the lacuna of German ghost stories. The *Gespensterbuch* (whose relevance to "Stumme Liebe" will be made clear shortly) was a salmagundi drawing on Orientalist motifs, French fairy tales, and Germanic folklore. In his foreword to the first volume, Laun speaks of how the anthology's title may lead 'friends of the Enlightenment' to expect 'lively

---

31 Richard Mercer Dorson, *History of British Folklore*, 2 (London and New York: Routledge, 2001), 1:109.
32 Walter Scott, 'On the Supernatural in Fictitious Composition and Particularly on the Works of Ernest Theodore William Hoffman', in *The Foreign Quarterly Review* 1 (July 1827): 70.
33 Scott, 'Supernatural in Fictitious Composition', 70
34 Scott, 'Supernatural in Fictitious Composition', 70.

pranks against religious belief and superstition'. Yet it may also appeal to those who trust in the existence of the realm of spirits; believers may even argue that the collection at hand provided 'a friendly aid' to their theories of ghosts.[35] Laun's unresolved wavering between refuting or validating ghostly manifestations is also borne out in the tales themselves. Some stories are what is called the 'explained supernatural' (i.e., they provide a natural explanation for what was first thought to be spectral appearances), while others seem to confirm the existence of apparitions.

In the afterword to the volume, Apel responds to what Max Weber would later name the *Entzauberung* (i.e. the 'disenchantment' or 'de-magic-ation') of the world. Apel holds that there may be another world beyond the horizon of the 'putative self-deluding Enlightenment' that rejects 'the marvellous', and he promotes the alternative of a *wahre Aufklärung* (true Enlightenment), which will expand the study of 'the marvelous' and truly attempt to 'comprehend' the supernatural.[36] However, he puts off the full investigation of the spiritual world to the arrival of 'a more enlightened time'.[37]

Gespensterbuch is relevant to the present discussion because "Stumme Liebe" was added to the collection when some of the stories were translated into French under the title of *Fantasmagoriana* (1812). The French translator was Jean-Baptiste Benoît Eyriès, otherwise known for his work as a geographer and as a translator of travel writing.[38] To make what is now "L'Amour muet" fit in with the other anonymous pieces, Musäus' name as the intermediary for the story is elided. Instead, the folktale is somewhat deceptively subtitled "Anecdote du seizième siècle" (anecdote of the sixteenth century), which obscures the fact that time and place in the tale had been added by Musäus, as he himself had made clear. More importantly, the French version is by no means a faithful translation of the tale. A great many details are left out, most notably the scholarly and worldly-wise commentaries are excised, and none of the five examples mentioned above survives. Thus, "L'Amour muet" comes across as folktale more in the line of what was published by the Brothers Grimm.

As with *Gespensterbuch*, Eyeriès' ontology of the spectral is not unambigious. The title of his collection echoes the 'phantasmagorias', which were shows

---

35 Laun, 'Vorrede', in *Gespensterbuch*, 5 vols., edited by Johann August Apel, Friedrich Laun (Leipzig: G.I. Göschen, 1811), 1:iii. My translation.
36 Apel, 'Nachrede', in *Gespensterbuch*, 1:285.
37 Apel, 'Nachrede', in *Gespensterbuch*, 1:286.
38 *Fantasmagoriana, ou recueil d'histoires d'apparitions de spectres, revenans, fantômes, etc.; traduit de l'allemand, par un Amateur* (Jean-Baptiste Benoît Eyriès) (Paris: F. Schoell, 1812). The stories translated were from the two first volumes of *Gespensterbuch*. Beyond, Musäus' story, there is also another tale not originally part of the German collection: "La chambre grise" ("Die graue Stube"), which was written by the German writer Heinrich Clauren.

performed in France since 1792 by Étienne-Gaspard Robert, a Belgian entertainer who had taken inspiration from the popular British Gothic novels. Robert used various projection techniques that created moving images by lighting them onto smoke, so they appeared as ghostly presences. But Eyriès sees the stories as more than just examples of illusions. In the preface, he emphasizes that, beyond the scope for amusement, ghost stories also give us access to ancient beliefs: 'it is proper that some repertory should exist, in which we may discover the traces of those superstitions to which mankind have so long been subject'.[39] Eyriès refers to the fact that ghosts are still believed by 'workmen in mines, and the inhabitants of mountainous countries'.[40] The reference here is to the Scottish writer Anne Grant's "Essays on the Superstitions of the Highlanders of Scotland", which was an early ethnographic investigation of superstition in a remote location of Britain.[41] But the belief in spirits was not only for the lower classes; Eyriès also refers to Emanuel Swedenborg, the eighteenth-century explainer of the spirit world; Louis Claude de Saint-Martin, the leading exponent of Illuminism; and Johann Heinrich Jung-Stilling's recent treatise *Theorie der Geister-Kunde* (1808) (Theory of spirit knowledge). Hence, the preface signals an interest in apparitions as a scientific object of enquiry, for which the ghost story would be one type of evidence.

Fantasmagoriana made an impact in Britain, as it was read by Lord Byron, his physician John Polidori, Mary Shelley, and P. B. Shelley, when this group decided to have a now famous ghost-storytelling contest at Villa Diodati, near Lake Geneva, in 1816. As a result of the competition, we now have Mary Shelley's *Frankenstein* (1818) and John Polidori's *The Vampyre* (1819).[42] But *Fantasmagoriana* was not just ambience to the story writing of others. Sarah Elizabeth Utterson translated five of the tales into English. Her volume entitled *Tales of the Dead* (1813) includes Musäus' story, now called "The Spectre-Barber". In the short 'Advertisement', Utterson notes that 'the passion for books of amusement founded on the marvellous relative to ghosts and spirits may be considered as having very much subsided' due to the numerous 'contemptible imitations' of Ann Radcliffe's Gothic novels that have inundated the book market.[43] In other words,

---

39 Jean-Baptiste Benoît Eyriès, "Préface du traducteur", in *Fantasmagoriana*, 2 vols., trans. J.-B. B. Eyriès (Paris: F. Schoell, 1812), 1:vii.
40 Eyriès, "Préface du traducteur", 1:xiii.
41 Anne Grant, "Essays on the Superstitions of the Highlanders of Scotland to which are added Translations from the Gaelic and Letters connected with those formerly published By the Author of Letters from the Mountains Mrs Grant Crown" (London: Longman et al. 1811).
42 For the influence of the *Fantasmagoriana* and its reception in this circle, see Maximiliaan van Woudenberg, "The Variants and Transformations of *Fantasmagoriana:* Tracing a Travelling Text to the Byron–Shelley Circle" *Romanticism* 20, no. 3 (2014): esp. 308.
43 Sarah Elizabeth Utterson, ed. and trans., *Tales of the Dead, Principally Translated from the French*, trans. Sarah Elizabeth Utterson (London: White, Cochrane and Co., 1813), i.

Utterson laments the fact that ghost stories have been commercialized as cheap thrills, rather than used as objects of study. She suggests that her translated collection will map the belief in ghosts that has dominated the 'Northern nations' where

> [the people] have been more the victims of credulity with respect to spirits [than the southern nations], they have indulged in the wanderings of fancy on subjects of this kind, and have eagerly employed their invention in forming narrations founded on the supposed communication between the spiritual world and mankind.[44]

Utterson's approach to the tales aligns in certain respects with a Herderian-Romantic celebration of folklore as embodying the authentic and irreducible characteristics of a nation or ethnic group. It is superstitious beliefs that command Utterson's interest. Therefore, she makes clear that "The Spectre-Barber" is a 'considerably curtailed' version of the French source, because the former version contained too much about Franz' love, which is misplaced in a collection of ghost stories.[45] If the French translation had already cut around one-fourth of Musäus' text, Utterson now reduces it to only one-third the length of the German original. The effect is that the nature of the story is entirely changed: it is no longer a meandering (literary) fairy tale, but a narrative primarily focused on the encounter with the ghost. The commentaries and literary flourishes that were superimposed upon the chronological order of events are left out altogether. Utterson further solidifies the association of "The Spectre-Barber" with vernacular tradition by prefacing it with a quote from the ballad known as "King Ryence's Challenge" (about the shaving of beards as a gesture of submission), which she would have found in Thomas Percy's antiquarian collection *Reliques of Ancient English Poetry* (1st edition. 1765).

It was as a work concerned with folkloristic superstitions that *Tales of the Dead* was reviewed in *The Quarterly Review* in 1820, alongside five other works – which included J. M. Thiele's collection of Danish folklore (1813), the Brothers Grimm's *German Legends* (1816), and L. F. von Dobeneck's *Des Deutschen Mittelalters Volksglauben Und Heroensagen* (1815) – all were gathered under the title "Popular Mythology of the Middle Ages". *Tales of the Dead* is included with these more philological editions on the grounds that the collection displays what the reviewer refers to as the 'imagination' of ghostlore.[46] For the reviewer, the desideratum for works dealing with folklore is that they must reach for the purest and most original source. Hence:

---

44 Utterson, *Tales of the Dead*, i.
45 Utterson, *Tales of the Dead*, ii.
46 Review 'Popular Mythology of the Middle Ages', in *The Quarterly Review* 43 (January 1820): 350.

> Tales of supernatural agency are not read to full advantage except in the authors by whom they are first recorded. When treated by moderns, much of their original character must necessarily evaporate; like tombs which lose their venerable sanctity when removed from the aisles of a cathedral and exposed in a museum.[47]

The reviewer further held that 'the attention of the reader is riveted' by 'the earnestness of ... credulity' found in writers of old.[48] Reading enjoyment thus correlated with the purity of the source. Following the logic of this evaluation, Musäus' stylistic overhaul of the story about the spectral barber would most certainly have been heavily criticized for obstructing readers' access to the past.

At the same time, the early nineteenth century was riven with debates about the function and obligation of literature. Not everyone bought into Romanticism's positive appraisal of folklore and irrational beliefs, especially not if such principles were seen to disregard the fear of God or destabilize established social norms. Some of these concerns were expressed in connection with another English translation of "Stumme Liebe" (entitled "The Spectre Barber"), which appeared in *Popular Tales and Romances of the Northern Nations* (1823). In the anonymous editor's preface, we are told that supernatural and fanciful stories 'form an important feature in the literature of the Germans, who seem to be the authenticated historians of Satan in all his varieties of name and attribute'.[49] Yet the editor also admonishes that 'fancy has had too much sway' with this people, and 'it has seldom been under the guidance of sound taste', for which reason 'the multitude of their original fictions is disgraced by the most babarous [sic] absurdities'.[50] This appears to be a comment that refers to the fact that 'German' had become almost a byword for terror-writing in the British book market.[51] The editor therefore applauds Musäus' presentation of the folktale 'under a light veil of irony, in a tone half jest, half earnest, and that is, indeed, its most beautiful form'.[52] "The Spectre Barber" is singled out as 'one of the happiest illustrations of this class of writing'.[53] Even if it excises many of Musäus' erudite comments, the translation maintains the humour and arms-length distance to the superstitious elements that Musäus had inserted. Musäus was seen in this evaluation as

---

47 "Popular Mythology", 349.
48 "Popular Mythology", 349.
49 n.a., "Preface" in *Popular Tales and Romances of the Northern Nations* (London: W. Simpkin and R. Marshall; and J. H. Bohte, 1823), 1:v.
50 n.a, "Preface", 1:ix.
51 Both the German *Schaurroman* and the terror-ballad had been successful in English translation. For a discussion of the influence of and reaction against these, see Silke Arnold-de Simine, "Blaming the Other: English Translations of Benedikte Naubert's Hermann von Unna (1788/1764)", in *The German Gothic and Its International Reception, 1800–2000*, ed. A. Cusack and B. Murnane (Rochester: Camden House, 2012), 60–75.
52 n.a, "Preface", 1:ix.
53 n.a, "Preface", 1:x.

showing the way for curating a folkish tradition. As Jason Marc Harris notes in his survey of nineteenth-century adaptations of folktales, we often find that the narration is packaged in a 'rhetoric of skepticism to distance the narrator from the beliefs of the non-elite'.[54]

Interest in folk tradition was also intrinsically linked with its satiric undoing in Matthew Gregory Lewis' two-volume *Ballads of Wonder* (1801). One volume has 28 traditional ghost ballads (several reprinted from Thomas Percy's *Reliques of Ancient English Poetry*), while the other has a mix of Lewis' own offerings, as well as imitations of folk ballads by Walter Scott, Robert Southey, and others. In particular, Lewis' new ballads are written in an idiom that teeters between the serious and the burlesque – some are unambiguously parodies, others are supercharged with terror tropes to such an extent that they become hyperbolic. Douglass H. Thomson, one of the modern editors of the collection, argues about the new contributions that 'Lewis ... uses parody to counter his critics' histrionic claims of its (the ballad's) damaging effect on audiences'.[55] In the Romantic period, making use of non-elite traditions was never straightforward; the baggage of irrationality and superstitious belief had to be carefully considered, and reassurances of the author's disengagement from the material was often necessary.

The Ghost Story as Haunted Site

Running contrary to the Romantic appropriation of "Stumme Liebe", an interest in Musäus' original satiric approach can be found in Thomas Roscoe's translation of the tale for the third volume of *The German Novelists* (1826). As the title indicates, Roscoe re-conceptualizes the tale (now entitled "The Dumb Lover") as essentially a novelistic prose story. There were several other translations of the story in the Victorian period with no clear interest in its origin in oral German tradition.[56] Here, I will briefly discuss what is best described as a free adaptation of "Stumme Liebe":

---

54 Jason Marc Harris, *Folklore and the Fantastic in Nineteenth-Century British Fiction* ((2008) London and New York: Routledge, 2016), 10.
55 Douglass H. Thomson, "Introduction", in Matthew Gregory Lewis, *Tales of Wonder* (Peterborough, ON: Broadview 2010), 15.
56 The novelist Arthur Sinclair included "The Spectre Barber – Partially Translated from the German of Musäus" in his *The Decameron of the West. A Series of Tales, &c.* (1839), an attempt to collect interesting stories from around the world. The publisher James Burns, who showed considerable interest in German literature, brought out a volume entitled *Select Popular Tales from the German of Musaeus* (1845), which presented seven tales, including "Mute Love". Some twenty years later, "Mute Love" was published in a translation by J. T. Hanstein, in *Popular Works of Musäus* (1865) and *The Chronicle of the Three Sisters and Mute Love* (1866), respectively.

the English journalist and novelist Dudley Costello's "Shaving a Ghost", included in his collection *Holidays with Hobgoblins* (1861). The publication was advertised as a 'Christmas Book' and included an engraving of the central shaving scene by the famous illustrator George Cruikshank.[57] Following Charles Dickens' hugely successful *A Christmas Carol. In Prose. Being a Ghost Story of Christmas* (first published in 1843), ghost stories at Christmas had become a lucrative market for publishers. It here seems that Costello's adaptation expands Musäus' project: using the ghost story as entertainment while making sure that the reader understands that any real belief in a marvellous universe was obsolete. In this sense, Costello instrumentalizes the notion of 'shaving a ghost' as a metaphor for cutting the supernatural down to size.

The scene is set around a castle placed near Boulogne-sur-Mer. This had been the home of the Scottish nobleman Yarl o'Tommietool, who had participated in the failed 1715 Jacobite rising to put the Stuarts on the British throne. O'Tommietool and his men had also wanted to participate in the later Jacobite insurrection of 1745, but never left France as there was too much fun to be had at home. In life, the spectral barber had been the Scottish lord's valet and now haunts the castle. As a ghost, he would shave those who foolishly spent the night there and gave them a good beating afterwards. Unaware of the castle's haunted history, the modern Scotsman Mr. MacGranite buys it as his property. One night, MacGranite finds himself under the ghost barber's razor, but afterwards he has the pluck to sit the ghost down and shave off his long beard in return. This procedure releases the ghost from his curse. There is no treasure to be found at the end of the story; the reward is rather that the ghost is expelled from the modern world. The ghost's power to frighten is shorn along with his beard. In fact, the ghostly is generally relegated to a hazy past. At the end of the story, we learn that the encounter survives only as a tall story with which MacGranite will regale others 'in moments of conviviality, when the whisky and toddy had gone its rounds', and listeners cannot make out whether it is told 'in jest or earnest'.[58] This conclusion in a homely atmosphere is a celebration of modernity – in which ghosts are only amusing stories.

"Shaving a Ghost" is the first item in Costello's *Holidays with Hobgoblins* and works as an allegory for the collection at large. That is to say, the attempt to neutralize the belief in spirits and the supernatural characterizes the pieces included in the book. Other humorous ghost stories, like "The Ghost of Pit Pond" and "The Apparition of Monsieur Bodry", are mixed in with analytical essays such as "Superstition and Traditions", in which Costello dismisses belief in the

---

57 Dudley Costello, *Holidays with Hobgoblins: And Talk of Strange Things* (London: John Camden Hotten, 1861).
58 Costello, *Holidays with Hobgoblins*, 21–22.

supernatural as 'the offspring of Ignorance and Fear'.[59] Nonetheless, such belief constitutes a hauntology (if I may borrow Jacques Derrida's term) that the modern world cannot entirely erase. The perseverance of superstition continues to rear its ugly head. What is at stake is encapsulated in the first lines of Costello's essay "Witchcraft and Old Boguey":

> About three or four years ago, the public learnt, from some communications which were made to the *Times* newspaper, that a belief in witchcraft still prevailed amongst the rural population of England. When, however, we find that such a belief is not confined to isolated cases, but is scattered broadcast over a whole district, it becomes the duty of all who have the education of the people at heart to lend their aid in endeavouring to extirpate a superstition as ridiculous as it is degrading.[60]

What is played out in the story of "The Ghost Barber" is a similar disruption of the modern nation's trajectory towards rationalism, in fact a threat to the stability of social order. MacGranite is appropriately a man who "throw(s) contempt upon all supernatural manifestations", and yet he is confronted with a ghost of the past, which he must actively banish.[61] It is significant that the ghostly barber in the story doubles as a spectre of Jacobite rebellion (he even appears in the recognizable breeches and velvet cap). Hence, the ghost symbolizes a threat to British society and its Protestant foundation: the ghost presents a hauntology in more ways than one.

Costello's *Holidays with Hobgoblins* reveals the difficulty of making light holiday entertainment out of stories of superstition when such superstition is seen as potentially disruptive of modern society. Carlyle defined this as a problem of literary genre with respect to Musäus' *Volksmärchen*. Musäus was the first to make use of the folktale as a 'mine of entertainment', but critics have subsequently 'lamented the incongruity between his subject and style' – by which we must understand the subject of the supernatural and the style of the secular, comic novel.[62] Whereas the traditional folktale needed no apology among its conventional audiences for the appearance of otherworldly agents, the modern ghost story was at war with itself. The problem was that preserving the logic of the supernatural tale while insisting on an ironic distancing from this very logic created discord.

We may at this point return to Musäus' original version of "Stumme Liebe". After the ghost has ceased his haunting, and Franz is to dig up the treasure chest that will restore his fortune, Musäus triumphs in the voice of the enlightened eighteenth century. The intrusive narrator rejoices in the fact that Franz needs no

---

59 Costello, *Holidays with Hobgoblins*, 45.
60 Costello, *Holidays with Hobgoblins*, 245–46.
61 Costello, *Holidays with Hobgoblins*, 12.
62 Carlyle, *German Romance*, 1:14.

blue light (*blaues Flämmlein*) (the usual symbol for the presence of a ghost) to unearth the buried riches, only a shovel. What we see here is Musäus releasing Franz from the supernatural yoke of the folktale, making him a hero of the modern novel who becomes the maker of his own destiny. Yet the reader is left somewhat puzzled, for Franz only knows where to find the treasure because the spectral barber had told him where to go. The incongruity between the novelistic voice and the logic of the folktale has led critic Laura Martin to pose an essential question about the logic of Musäus' *Volkmärchen:* 'Should one spurn superstition in favor of modern science, or should one take on the happy-go-lucky attitude of the fairy-tale hero to whom all things come if only he accepts the gift freely?'.[63] The marvellous story world of the folktale is inevitably at some distance from a post-Enlightenment understanding of the universe, but any measure of satiric commentary cannot annul the supernatural logic inherent in the folktale. This makes Musäus' "Stumme Liebe" a fundamentally unstable text.

Conclusion

There is little doubt that Musäus saw himself as a modernist. In the literary system of the eighteenth century, genre was a mould that ensured cultural approval, and Musäus was able to introduce a low genre to a polite reading public by adapting the folktale with elements borrowed from the comic novel. By introducing humorous observations on events (only to be enjoyed by those middle-class readers who possess enough learning to appreciate the jokes), Musäus distances his readers from the vulgar superstitions of the oral original. Although often ignored today, Musäus helped spark an interest in folktales. His satiric repackaging of oral tradition made the folktale relevant to a readership of the 1780s. The folklorists Iona and Peter Opie note that literary retellings should not be seen as the destruction of the folktales, rather literary adaptations often secured their survival, and they are likely 'to have acquired fresh significance, as they passed through sophisticated communities'.[64] But relocating the folktale to a new medium and adapting it for a new audience was not unproblematic. It has been my argument that "Stumme Liebe" became an unsteady textual construct, as Musäus exploited the dramatic pleasure of the folktale while signalling through satire that he does not surrender to its retrograde irrationality.

---

63 Laura Martin "Review: Malgorzata Kubisiak's *Märchen und Meta-Märchen*", in *Marvels & Tales* 18, no. 1 (2004): 134.
64 Iona Archibald Opie, Peter Opie, *The Classic Fairy Tales* (Oxford: Oxford University Press, 1974), 17.

The trajectory of "Stumme Liebe", as it moved across borders in printed form, shows us that the folktale did not stop its evolution when it was taken up by literate culture. Rather it was the simpler and pared-down versions that excited readers in the early nineteenth century. Utterson's and Eyriès renditions were not just an indication that aesthetic preferences shifted in the Romantic period; they also gave the folktale and its conceptual framework of the marvellous a new legitimacy. However, if these extractions of the basic storyline presumed to return the story to its original state, they were, in fact, no less artificial constructs than Musäus' stylish remake of the folktale. In late eighteenth and early nineteenth centuries, as the folktale was coming into its own as a genre, it was constantly negotiated, undone, redone, and repaired.

Anthony Apesos
(Lesley University)

Visionary Anatomy: Blake's Bodies

Abstract
The human figure is the central subject of William Blake's prints and drawings, but he rarely depicts the arrangement of the musculature of the body with anatomical accuracy. Here, I will explore the origin and significance of Blake's divergence from anatomical correctness. I hope to demonstrate that the incorrect anatomy of William Blake's figures is a subversion of the mechanistic view of the body that is consistent with his rejection of the mechanistic understanding of the world of Newtonian physics and Deistic theology. Further, I will suggest how Blake's anti-mechanistic beliefs bear on his views on universal forgiveness.

Keywords
Figure drawing, William Hunter, Joshua Reynolds, Royal Academy, Luigi Schiavonetti

Although William Blake's paintings and prints are peopled with naked male and female figures, Blake rarely depicts the arrangement of the musculature of the human body with anatomical accuracy. Some of his pictures, like his several versions of the Last Judgement, swarm with bodies, mostly naked, in a synchronized flow. Others, like *Albion Rose,* also known as *Glad Day* (ill. 1) show the naked figure alone in the landscape or in an interior as in *The Ghost of a Flea*. With so many nudes in his work, Blake had innumerable occasions to consider the structure of the human body, but when he occasionally depicts figures with correct anatomy often it seems to be by accident. This indifference is in strong contrast to the passion for accurate anatomical knowledge exhibited by many of his contemporaries.[1] Here I will analyze how Blake constructed his figures and compare them to the morphology of figures in the works of his contemporaries. Then I will try to understand the origin and significance of Blake's divergence from anatomical correctness. Finally, I hope to demonstrate that the incorrect anatomy of William Blake's figures is a subversion of the mechanistic view of the

---

[1] Stephanie Adair Rispoli, "Anatomy, Vitality, and the Romantic Body: Blake, Coleridge and the Hunter Circle, 1750–1840" (PhD diss., University of North Carolina, 2013), 84.

body that is consistent with his rejection of the mechanistic understanding of the world of Newtonian physics and deistic theology.

Figure 1. William Blake, *Albion Arose (Glad Day)*, c. 1803–10. Engraving, 10 5/8 x 7 5/8 in, National Gallery of Art, Washington. Rosenwald Collection. Photo: https://www.nga.gov/collec tion/art-object-page.11492.html.

As is well known, Blake's style of figure drawing was derived from sixteenth century central Italian painting, especially the work of Michelangelo and Raphael, with emphasis on the former.[2] Already as an apprentice he collected prints after Michelangelo, Raphael, Giulio Romano, and original prints by Albrecht

---

[2] Among the many authors who have discussed this are Bindman, Blunt, and Raine. See David Bindman, *Blake as an Artist* (Oxford: Phaidon, 1977); Anthony Blunt, *The Art of William Blake* (New York: Columbia University Press, 1959) and Kathleen Raine, *William Blake* (New York: Praeger, 1971).

Durer and Martin van Heemskerck and rejected engravings after the likes of Titian, Antonio da Correggio, Peter Paul Rubens,[3] and even original etchings by Rembrandt. Because of his enthusiasm for collecting and the discernment in his choices, one print dealer, whose shop Blake frequented, called him his "young connoisseur".[4] In 1779, Blake enrolled in the Royal Academy while it was directed by its first president Sir Joshua Reynolds. Years later, in his copy of Reynolds's *Discourses on Art*, Blake wrote, among many other annotations, the following recollection:

> I was once looking over the Prints from Rafael & Michael Angelo. in the Library of the Royal Academy Moser [the academy's keeper] came to me & said You should not Study these old Hard Stiff & Dry Unfinishd Works of Art, Stay a little & I will shew you what you should Study. He then went & took down Le Bruns & Rubens's Galleries How I did secretly Rage. I also spoke my mind. I said to Moser, These things that you call Finishd are not Even Begun how can they then, be Finishd? The Man who does not know The Beginning, never can know the End of Art.[5]

Comparison of examples of engravings, like those Blake was studying, with those that Moser might have offered him as superior alternatives show what Blake valued and what he derided. For instance, in a Marcantonio Raimondi print after Raphael (ill. 2), we see a fine mesh of lines that never obscure the edges of the figures, whereas in the copy by Henrik Severs after Rubens (ill. 3) we see an emphasis on the general pattern of light and dark that holds the figures together into unified masses. The Severs print also exhibits long cross contour lines that assist in stressing the general volumetric form of the figure as is seen over the chest of the figure in the detail (ill. 4). The lines in the Marcantonio print as shown in the detail (ill. 5), are finer and more responsive to the particular local typographies of the torso of the figure. For Blake, in prints like Severs's copy after Rubens, the outline, which Blake considered to be the starting point in depicting the figure, is lost.[6]

Artists like Rubens used oil paint to create pictures, and Blake believed that it was the very nature of oil paint that afforded this loss of outline. Alexander

---

[3] Benjamin Heath Malkin, "From 'A Father's Memoirs of His Child'", ed. Arthur Symons (London: A. Constable, 1907 [1806]), 313.
[4] Malkin, "From 'A Father's Memoirs of His Child'", 313.
[5] William Blake, David V. Erdman and Harold Bloom, *The Complete Poetry and Prose of William Blake. Newly rev. ed.* (Garden City, N.Y.: Anchor Books, 1982), 639.
[6] Blake would also have been prejudiced against the print after Rubens by the nature of the engraved lines themselves which swell and taper. Blake acquired, in his apprenticeship to the engraver James Basire (1730–1802), a technique of thin lines like those in the Marcantonio Raimondi print. See Robert N. Essick, *William Blake, Printmaker* (Princeton, N.J.: Princeton University Press, 1980). This approach to engraving remained the method that Blake held to throughout his life and is most beautifully demonstrated in his late masterpiece, the engraved illustrations to the Book of Job.

Figure 2. Marcantonio Raimondi, *The Massacre of the Innocents*, c. 1512–13. Engraving, 28.1 x 43.0 cm, Metropolitan Museum, New York. Photo: https://www.metmuseum.org/art/collection/search/342748.

Gilchrist, Blake's biographer who interviewed his subject's surviving contemporaries, reports that:

> Blake used to tell of an interview he had once had with Reynolds, in which our neglected enthusiast found the originator of a sect in art, to which his own was so hostile very pleasant personally, as most found him. "Well, Mr. Blake," blandly remarked the President, who, doubtless, had heard strange accounts of his interlocutor's sayings and doings, "I hear you despise our art of oil-painting." "No, Sir Joshua, I don't despise it; but I like fresco better."[7]

Blake's opinion of fresco was based on the engravings after artists he admired while his understanding of oil painting was founded on contact with the practice of painters like his English contemporaries Reynolds and Thomas Gainsborough. Their paintings show lost edges, soft focus, and open brush work that allowed the figure to merge with its surroundings. Blake believed the very slow drying time of oil paint and the practice of using it on canvas made these qualities, often termed "painterly," difficult to escape (ill. 6 and 7).[8]

---

7 Alexander Gilchrist and Anne Gilchrist, *Life of William Blake, with Selections from His Poems and Other Writings. Volume I. A new and enl. ed* (London: Macmillan and Co., 1880), 95.

8 Blake must have seen panel paintings in oil by some of those fresco painters he admired that did not have such painterly qualities. Blake would not have missed visiting the well attended sale exhibitions of old master paintings from the Orléans Collection held in London in 1793 and

Figure 3. Henrik Severs after P. P. Rubens, *Virgin Enthroned with Child and Saints*. Engraving. Art market, location unknown.

1798, but he must not have recognized that, for example, the several fine Raphael's Madonnas in those exhibitions were painted in the medium that he claimed not to despise but for which he certainly had no enthusiasm. For more on the Orléans collection in London see Julia Arm-

Figure 4. Detail of 3.

Figure 5. Detail of 2.

Reynolds, before he retired as president of the Academy, declared that the last word he wanted to utter in his last discourse to the students and members was to be the name "Michelangelo". Despite this token of admiration to Blake's hero, it did not disguise for Blake that Reynold's own approach to painting was derived not from the Florentine master but from the technique of those very artists – Titian, Rubens, and Rembrandt – that Blake rejected.

As a student in the Royal Academy, Blake would have been exposed to other views of painting besides the painterly aesthetic promoted at the academy by its president. He would have been expected, if not required, to attend lectures by professors and to meet with established artists designated as "visitors". The most illustrious of the professors was the anatomist William Hunter, the elder brother of another famous anatomist and surgeon, John Hunter. Blake parodied the younger Hunter in his early satire *An Island in the Moon* (1784), but whether Blake was personally acquainted with John Hunter beyond a knowledge of his

---

strong-Totten, "The Orléans Phenomenon in Great Britain" in The Orléans Collection, ed. Vanessa I. Schmid (Lewes, UK: New Orleans Museum and D. Giles Ltd, 2019), 191–201.

Figure 6. Joshua Reynolds, *Portrait of Captain George K. H. Coussmaker*, 1782. Oil on canvas, 238.1 x 145.4 cm. Metropolitan Museum, New York. Photo: https://www.metmuseum.org/art/collection/search/437447.

Figure 7. Detail of figure 6.

reputation is disputed; however, Blake certainly would have attended William Hunter's lectures at the Academy.[9] In these lectures, Hunter had on hand to illustrate his teaching a live male model, a skeleton, an écorché figure, and a cadaver. This latter prop he would dissect to show the attachment of muscles to bones so the students could understand the mechanism of human movement.[10] Hunter stressed the necessity of thorough anatomical knowledge for the artist. Without such knowledge, he believed that the artist cannot depict the human figure with the accuracy necessary for the expression of emotions. Hunter maintained that 'in Fine Arts the more precise the imitation of Nature is that is the nearer we come to the point of realizing [Nature] the more striking I would suppose the effect to be; and therefore the more pleasing'.[11] And that

> from these general observations it appears that in Painting and Sculpture the power of representing the human body in all the variety of its circumstances as near as possible to the original reality must be an acquisition of the greatest consequence, because it is so essential to the effect of the work. If there be but a single transgression it strikes a correct eye, disturbing the imagination, and like an absurd Player in a moving scene, breaks the charm; the sweet delusion vanishes, and nothing is left but canvas lines and colours.[12]

To be able to avoid any transgression of accuracy the artist must understand the physical nature of the body which Hunter likens to a machine:

> Let us observe that the variety of the positions and of the form of the whole body and of its several parts depends principally upon the state of the internal parts, particularly of the bones and muscles. These are covered with more or less of fat and the whole is wrapped up in a thin sheet we call skin. The internal parts change their figure and situation in a number of ways and thereby produce the wonderful variety which we see accurately brought out in living bodies, now to illustrate our subject let us suppose there is some mechanical machine to which we mean to compare the human body made up of pieces which move on one another so as to produce a great variety in the external figure and position of the machine.[13]

This machine works though a rational relation of its parts:

---

9 Jane M. Oppenheimer, "A Note on William Blake and Allied Sciences", *Journal of the History of Medicine and Allied Arts* 1, no.1 (1946): 41–45. https://doi.org/10.1093/jhmas/1.1.41.

10 For more on the teaching of Hunter at the Academy time, see Oppenheimer, "A Note", 41–45; William Hunter and Martin Kemp, *Dr. William Hunter at the Royal Academy of Arts* (Glasgow: University of Glasgow Press, 1975); Rispoli, "Anatomy, Vitality, and the Romantic Body", 84; Anne Dulau Beveridge, "The Anatomist and the Artists: Hunter's Involvement" in *William Hunter's World*, ed. Nicholas Pearce E. Geoffrey Hancock, and Mungo Campbell (London: Routledge, 2015), 81–95; Annette Wickham, "Anatomical Studies." in *The Royal Academy of Arts: History and Collections*, ed. Robin Simon with Maryanne Stevens (New Haven: Yale University Press, 2018), 506–523.

11 Hunter and Kemp, *Dr. William Hunter*, 38.

12 Hunter and Kemp, *Dr. William Hunter*, 41.

13 Hunter and Kemp, *Dr. William Hunter*, 32.

> Muscles are the masses of red fibrous flesh / which by a particular power of contracting or shortening are the immediate agents and causes of all our motions. The greatest part of the system is fastened to the bones and served to move them in a variety of different positions.
>
> The study of the bones and muscles will allow to be very essential to painters and sculptors if it be known and it is really true that every variety which every living creature can bring out depends upon the play of muscles every varied attitude action and gesture every change of faith is no other than varied muscular motion everything that we have seen acted in reality ... is nothing but a skillful exercise of muscular motion.[14]

Martin Kemp has compared Hunter's views on anatomy to those of Joshua Reynolds, and he explains that Reynolds did not believe that the study of anatomy need lead to the kind of anatomical precision that Hunter promoted. Instead for Reynolds, familiarity with structure of the body would give an artist an understanding with which to create a generalized ideal of the body consistent with Reynold's painterly aesthetic.[15]

Since Blake opposed the painterly painting promoted by the Academy's president, one might think that William Hunter's belief in the importance of as perfect-as-possible accuracy gained through anatomical study would have appealed to him. Instead, Blake's writings prove that Hunter's attitude towards art would have been perhaps even more offensive to Blake's strongest held beliefs. For Blake, the bodily functions are not mechanical, as Hunter taught, but miraculous:

> We who dwell on Earth can do nothing of ourselves, every thing is conducted by Spirits, no less than Digestion or Sleep.[16]

And:

> ... every Natural Effect has a Spiritual Cause, and Not
> A Natural: for a Natural Cause only seems, it is a Delusion
> Of Ulro: & a ratio of the perishing Vegetable Memory.[17]

In respond to Hume's statement that 'A miracle is a violation of the laws of nature', Blake would insist that such violations pervade the natural world.[18] As to the study of anatomy by dissection, Blake was clearly horrified:

> Why wilt thou Examine every little fibre of my soul
> Spreading them out before the Sun like Stalks of flax to dry

---

14 Hunter and Kemp, *Dr. William Hunter*, 36-37.
15 Martin Kemp, "True to Their Natures: Sir Joshua Reynolds and Dr. William Hunter at The Royal Academy of Arts", *Notes and Records of the Royal Society of London* 46, no. 1 (1992): 77-88.
16 Blake, Erdman and Bloom, *Complete Poetry and Prose*, 145.
17 Blake, Erdman and Bloom, *Complete Poetry and Prose*, 124.
18 John Locke et. al, *The empiricists* (New York: Anchor Books; Doubleday, 1990), 391.

> The infant joy is beautiful but its anatomy
> Horrible Ghast & Deadly nought shalt thou find in it
> But Death Despair & Everlasting brooding Melancholy[19]

Blake's repulsion would have not only been generated by Hunter's demonstrations on cadavers but also by the vivid anatomical illustrations in William Cowper's *Anatomy of the Humane Bodies* (1698) and William Hunter's *The Anatomy of the Human Gravid Uterus Exhibited in Figures* (1774).[20] Both were very well known, and Blake as a professional engraver would have been very interested in the striking engravings in both books. The illustration of the circulatory system in the earlier book (ill. 8) certainly seems to have inspired the lines, "every little fibre of my soul / Spreading them out before the Sun like Stalks of flax to dry." In his early satire *An Island in the Moon* (1784), Blake's satirical caricature of John Hunter, William Hunter's brother, as Jack Tearguts, reveals an antipathy to anatomical study:

> He understands anatomy better than any of the Ancients. He'll plunge his knife up to the hilt in a single drive and thrust his fist in, and all in the space of a Quarter of an hour. he does not mind their crying—tho they cry ever so. He'll Swear at them & keep them down with his fist & tell them that he'll scrape their bones if they don't lay still & be quiet[21]

Even though we have no record of Blake directly commenting on William Hunter's lectures on the body, it is impossible not to conclude that Blake would have seen Hunter's teaching as consistent with the mechanistic worldview that he rejected. He repeatedly condemns Francis Bacon, Isaac Newton, and John Locke, as three thinkers to whom he ascribes the mechanistic clockwork theory of the cosmos.[22] Blake's antagonism towards this mechanistic view of the world pervades his writing and is seen already in his earliest illuminated book in which he rejects the rationalism of natural religion, also known as deism:

> I. Mans perceptions are not bounded by organs of perception. he percieves more than sense (tho' ever so acute) can discover.

---

19 Blake, Erdman and Bloom, *Complete Poetry and Prose*, 167.
20 Tristanne J. Connolly, *William Blake and the Body* (Houndmills, Basingstoke, Hampshire and New York: Palgrave Macmillan, 2002) 46–47. Cowper's book was notorious for having taken illustrations, without acknowledgement from Govard Bidloo *Anatomia Humani Corporis* (Amsterdam, 1685) with plates by Gérard de Lairesse. Note that the illustration here is original to Cowper's publication.
21 Blake, Erdman and Bloom, *Complete Poetry and Prose*, 454 – I added some punctuation.
22 Bryce J. Christensen, "The Apple in the Vortex: Newton, Blake and Descartes", *Philosophy and Literature* 6, no. 1 & 2 (Fall 1982): 147–161. https://doi.org/10.1353/phl.1982.0004. Bryce argues that Newton was not the materialist as he was understood to be by Blake and his contemporaries. Newton was indeed rather more of a mystic "whose natural philosophy [was twisted] into a thoroughly mechanistic system". Christensen, "The Apple in the Vortex", 152.

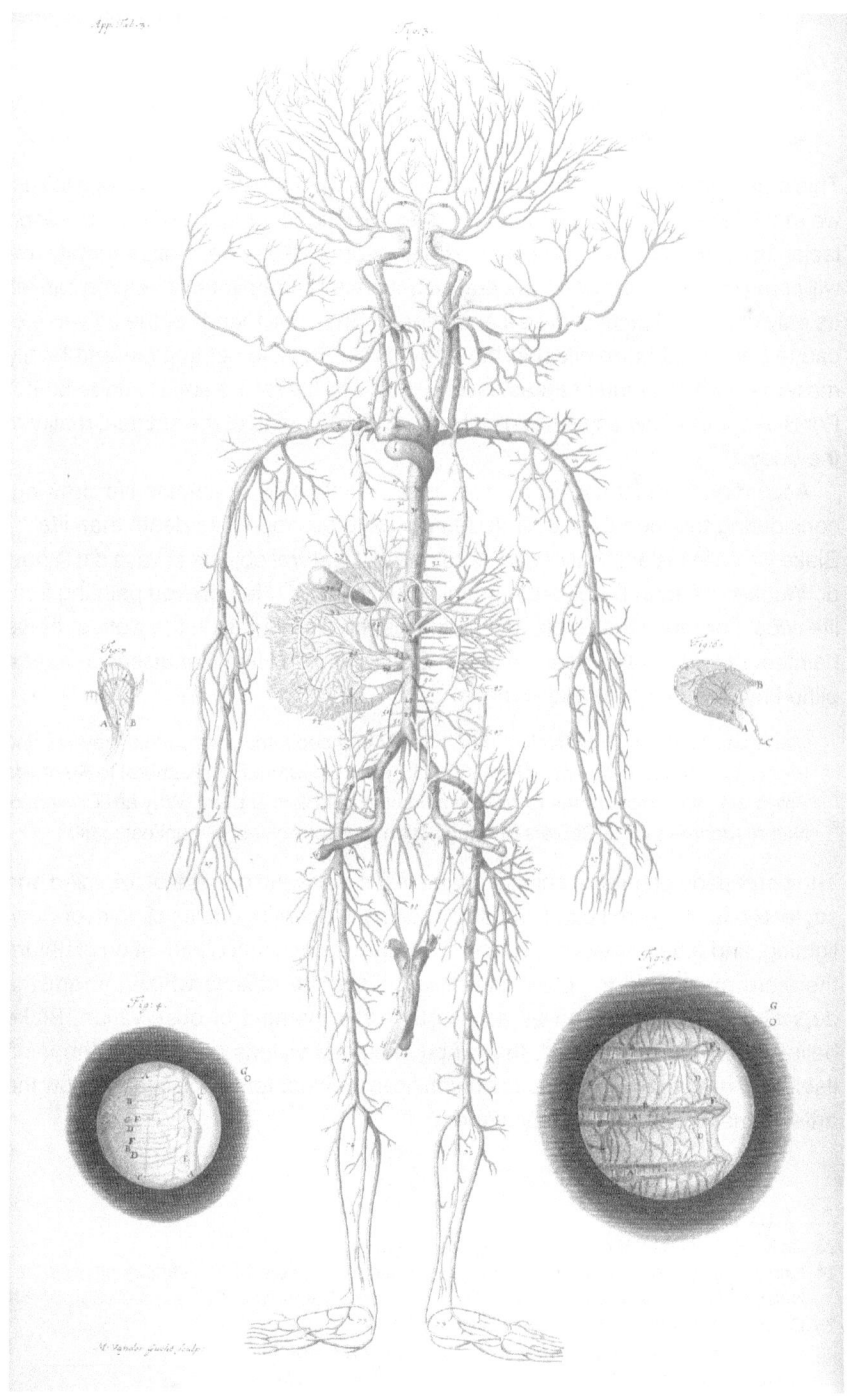

Figure 8. Michiel van der Gucht. Engraving after Henry Cook, *Arterial system.* Appendix Table 3 from William Cowper, *The Anatomy of Humane Bodies.* London, 1698. Wellcome Collection.

II. Reason or the ratio of all we have already known. is not the same that it shall be when we know more.

[III. lacking]

IV. The bounded is loathed by its possessor. The same dull round even of a univer [s] e would soon become a mill with complicated wheels.[23]

This argument can be paraphrased: When we know more than the senses tell us, we must see that reason is bound to sense experience. Being so bound, reason lacks the competence to deal with extrasensory knowledge. Consequently, we will come to hate reason after we realize because of its limitations, reason can tell us only of the dull facts of cause and effect.[24] The "dull round" of the universe of cause and effect is manifest in the body as the muscle contraction and bodily movement which Hunter saw as essential knowledge for the artist to understand. For Blake, this knowledge is instead a misunderstanding of the spiritual reality of the body.

According to Gilchrist, Blake was even repelled by academic life drawing, considering the models in their frozen poses to be "more like death than life".[25] Blake wrote in his annotations to Wordsworth, "Natural objects always did & now do Weaken deaden & obliterate Imagination in Me".[26] He believed painting from life, would produce the "blots and blurs" that he disparaged in the work of those painters outside of the tradition of the Central Italian High Renaissance exemplified by Michelangelo and Raphael:

> Men think they can Copy Nature as Correctly as I copy Imagination this they will find Impossible. & all the Copies or Pretended Copiers of Nature from Rembrat to Reynolds Prove that Nature becomes to its Victim nothing but Blots & Blurs. Why are Copiers of Nature Incorrect while Copiers of Imagination are Correct this is manifest to all[27]

The perception of natural objects originates in the world outside of the mind and so, for Blake, they are soiled and deformed by the contingencies of point of view, lighting, and other unessential factors. Drawing from direct observation of nature therefore must yield to "blots and blurs," since the objects which the artist is depicting are so obscured by accidents in the moment of observation. Blake believed, on the other hand, that since imagined visions originate in the mind itself they are untainted by factors extrinsic to their content and so must allow the artist to make clear depictions of them.

---

23 Blake, Erdman and Bloom, *Complete Poetry and Prose*, 2.
24 Nelson Hilton argues that Blake's anti-materialism is prophetic of 20th century physics. See Nelson Hilton, "Blake and the Perception of Science", *Annals of Science* 4 (1986): 54–68.
25 Gilchrist and Gilchrist, *Life of William Blake*, 30.
26 Blake, Erdman and Bloom, *Complete Poetry and Prose*. 665.
27 Blake, Erdman and Bloom, *Complete Poetry and Prose*, 574–5.

Christopher Heppner notes Blake's anatomical incorrectness and ascribes it to Blake's avoidance of drawing from direct observation. Heppner's discussion of Blake's figure drawing leads him to compare Blake's depictions of the body to Michelangelo's. According to Heppner, Michelangelo's means of expression requires "he interplay between tension and relaxation, an interplay that depends upon a profound understanding of the workings of the human body to communicate exact states of feeling and intention."[28] Further he writes Michelangelo's "very muscle tone communicates subtle feelings by kinaesthetic empathy."[29] These statements express the same view of anatomy that we find in Hunter's lectures. According to Heppner, to achieve in his work what we find in Michelangelo's, Blake "would have had to learn anatomy in a serious way. He would have had to spend years in life class."[30] The errors in Blake's anatomy are so extreme and pervasive that they do not reveal a lack of serious effort but instead suggest the presence of a very serious rejection not only of life drawing but of Hunter's materialistic discussion of the body. By these errors I do not mean distortions in proportion or extreme poses. J. R. Harvey provides an analysis of *The Body of Abel Found by Adam and Eve* (ill. 9) and complains about the disproportionate legs of the running Cain, which he says appear to come from two figures of different stature.[31] These distortions are not errors of anatomy but exaggerations of proportions that are clearly employed for expressive reasons: the longer extended leg propelled Cain forward while, paradoxically seeming to drag him back, and the shorter leg on the ground seems to anchor his body preventing it from acceleration. This is the kind of distortion that is pervasive in the works of Henry Fuseli. Blake often referred to himself as a student of Fuseli[32]; Fuseli returned the compliment in saying "Blake is d – good to steal from. "[33], but as anatomists they are very different. Fuseli, like Blake in the example of the running figure of Cain, distorts proportions, for expressive purposes. Fuseli also exaggerates muscles and simplifies them. The peculiar errors in Blake's anatomy are of a very different kind.

To show the nature of these errors I will anatomize several of Blake's figures, but before proceeding, a basic understanding of the mechanism of the skeletal-muscular system that Hunter discussed in his lectures is necessary. In all ver-

---

28 Christopher Heppner, *Reading Blake's Designs* (Cambridge; New York: Cambridge University Press, 1995), 48.
29 Heppner, *Reading Blake's Designs*, 53.
30 Heppner, *Reading Blake's Designs*, 54. Does Heppner believe *anyone* would need "years in life class" to master anatomy? Or does he think *Blake* was especially dense and would have needed such extended study? Either way, he is mistaken.
31 147.
32 Raymond Lister, *William Blake* (London: Harper Collins, 1968),138.
33 Jean Hagstrum, *William Blake: Poet and Painter* (Chicago: University of Chicago Press, 1978), 67.

Figure 9. William Blake, *The Body of Abel Found by Adam and Eve,* 1826. Ink, tempera and gold on mahogany, 367 × 473 mm, Tate Gallery, London. Photo: © Tate https://www.tate.org.uk/art/artworks/blake-the-body-of-abel-found-by-adam-and-eve-n05888.

tebrates, all willed changes in posture and location of the body are caused by the combined contraction and relaxation of muscular pairs called antagonists. Each muscle in these pairs is attached to the skeleton. The attachment closer in proximity to the core of the body are called the *origin* of the muscle and the other end, the distal attachment, is called the *insertion.* The tissues that attach muscle to the bone are called *tendons*. The bones are attached to each other at the joint by a tough flexible tissue called *ligament.*

Illustration 10 shows the simplest possible arrangement of these tissues in which the contraction of one muscle, accompanied by the relaxation of its antagonist, causes a joint to bend; conversely, the relaxation of that muscle and the contraction of the antagonist realigns the bones, straightening the joint. The particulars of the arrangement vary throughout the body but not the principle. Sometimes the muscle has more than one origin and the origin may not be on a bone that is closest to the joint that is moved; for example, the biceps muscle originates at both the scapula and the humerus. The length of the tendons can be longer or shorter in ratio to the length of the muscle; for example, the deltoid muscle which originates on three bones has a tendinous attachment to them that is so abbreviated that it may seem as though the muscle is directly adhered to the

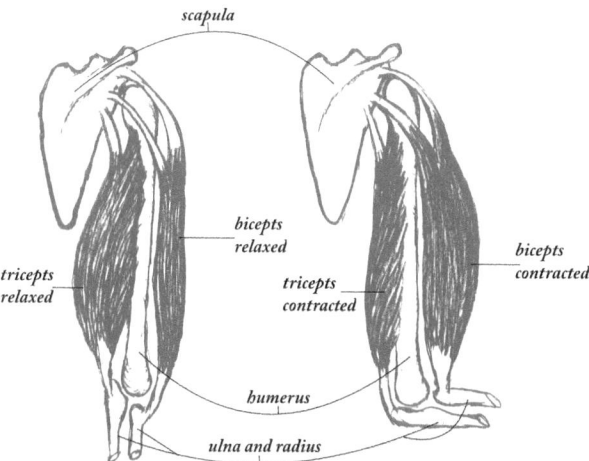

Figure 10. Diagram of antagonistic muscles of the elbow. Right, contraction bends joint. Left, contraction straightens joint.

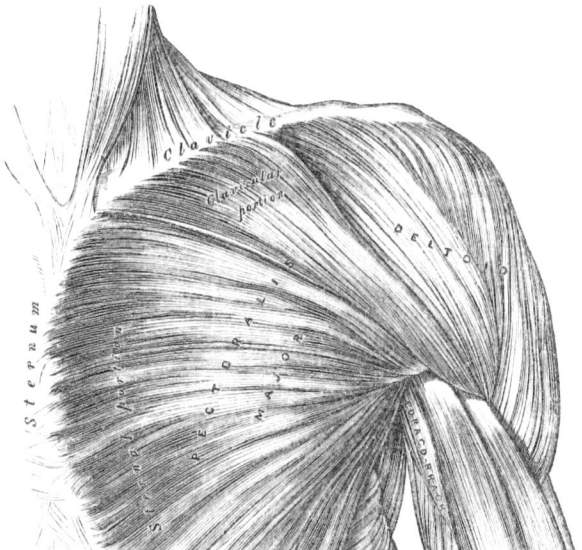

Figure 11. Henry Vandyke Carter, *Muscles of the Chest*, Plate 169. Wood engraving. *Gray's Anatomy* 1860. Wellcome Collection.

bones. In the illustrations of the shoulder girdle (ill. 11 and 12), it is important to notice that some bony surfaces are subcutaneous; no matter the degree of fat or muscular development of the individual figure these bones are only covered by skin. If an individual's body is fleshier in fat or muscle, the subcutaneous bones present as indentations in the body, while in an emaciated body, the subcuta-

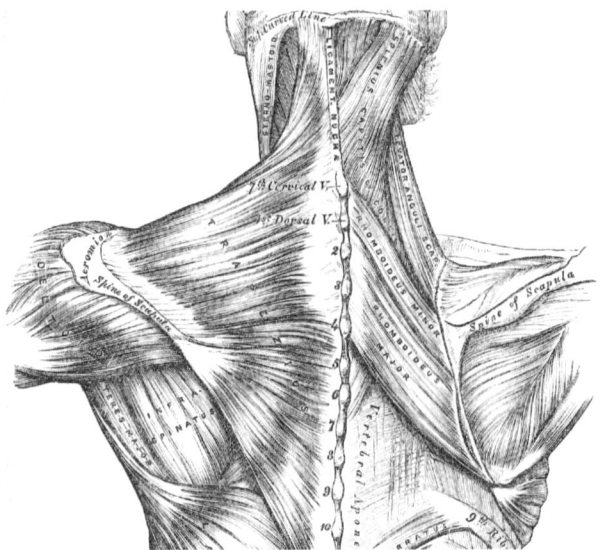

Figure 12. Henry Vandyke Carter, *Muscles of the Back*, detail of Plate 160. Wood engraving. *Gray's Anatomy* 1860. Wellcome Collection.

neous bones are prominent as bumps or ridges. The relation of muscles to these bones and the overlapping of muscles are consistently arranged in normal individual bodies of the same species regardless of muscular development.[34]

We see the facts of bodily architecture in the work of one of Blake's contemporaries who Blake particularly admired. In the right shoulder of Zeus from James Barry's *Birth of Pandora* (figure ill. 13), the muscles are represented as they are in a human body: The deltoid muscle originates at the clavicle and the acromion process of the scapula and then narrows to disappear between the biceps and triceps where it is inserted onto the humerus. The biceps muscle emerges from the armpit beneath the pectoral muscle which itself is inserted between the biceps and the deltoid onto the humerus. The clavicle is obscured by a lock of Zeus' black hair, yet the angle of the bone rising at a gentle angle from the top of the sternum to its meeting at the acromion is nonetheless discernible. The clavicle of the left shoulder is more visible as each end of it emerges from the shadow cast over it. By contrast to Barry's depiction, one can search the shoulders of Blake's *Albion Rose* (ill. 1) and will scarcely find any of these anatomical features.

The clarity of Blake's work makes it easy to dissect the anatomy of his figures and to compare that anatomy to the engravings after the masters he collected, to the works of his contemporaries, and to the anatomy of the living human body. As

---

34 Anthony Apesos, *Anatomy for Artists* (Cincinnati: Northlight Books, 2007), 14–16.

Figure 13. James Barry, detail of *Birth of Pandora*, 1791–1804. Oil on canvas, h 279 x w 520 cm, Manchester Art Gallery, Manchester. Photo: Manchester Art Gallery, UK © Manchester Art Gallery/Bridgeman Images. https://artuk.org/discover/artworks/the-birth-of-pandora-204422.

Figure 13a. James Barry, *Birth of Pandora*, 1791–1804. Oil on canvas, h 279 x w 520 cm, Manchester Art Gallery, Manchester. Photo: Manchester Art Gallery, UK © Manchester Art Gallery/Bridgeman Images. https://artuk.org/discover/artworks/the-birth-of-pandora-204422.

Connolly notes, Blake's bodies unnaturally emphasize skin clinging to the muscles revealing their shape and that even clothing clinging "to the body [reveals] its shape so much so that they seem to be part of the body growing out of it, failing to serve the purpose of covering it."[35]

In Blake's early drawings after Giorgio Ghisi's engravings of Michelangelo's Sistine Chapel ceiling, we find that Blake neither follows his sources nor con-

---

35 Connolly, *William Blake and the Body*, 45.

Figure 14. Giorgio Ghisi, detail from *The Persian Sibyl; from the series of Prophets and Sibyls in the Sistine Chapel*, 1570–75. Engraving, 55.8 × 41.3 cm. Metropolitan Museum, New York. Photo: https://www.metmuseum.org/art/collection/search/367702.

sistently alters them.[36] Blake somewhat improves Ghisi's depiction of the proximal end of the deltoid; in Ghisi's engraving of Abijah (ill. 14) we see it as a blunted form, and in Blake's copy (ill. 15), it shows some reasonable resemblance to its origin at the spine of the scapula. But while Ghisi shows the correct insertion of the deltoid between the triceps and biceps, Blake pulls the deltoid to a point where the insertion is undecipherable. The bumps that form a ring around the shoulder blade in Ghisi, Blake has translated into something more fleshlike, but they still have no correspondence to features in the human body. The many other engravings after Michelangelo that Blake would have seen and possibly collected are no more correct than Ghisi's. For example, the several engravings

---

36 Jenijoy La Belle discusses these drawings but without a sufficient regard to anatomy to clarify the differences between Blake's copies and Ghisi's engravings. La Belle says (would advise "writes" instead of "says"), "Blake copied Ghisi with great exactness." As I show, this is not the case. See Jenijoy La Belle, "Blake's Visions and Revisions of Michelangelo" in *Blake in His Time*, ed. Robert N. Essick and Donald Pearce (Bloomington: Indiana University Press, 1978), 13.

Figure 15. William Blake, copy after Ghisi, *Abijah*. Drawing. Verso, British Museum, Photo: © British Museum.

after the Sistine Chapel's *Last Judgement* show mostly figures with unintelligible marks that do not represent the anatomy of the mostly very accurate figures by Michelangelo.

Had Blake learned anatomy only from Ghisi and the other prints that he collected, the odd anatomy of his work could be explained, but Blake's knowledge of the human form was not so rudimentary. The constitution of the Academy of 1768 is explicit about the requirements that drawings be submitted for consideration for enrollment, and surely, anatomical correctness would have been a criterion that the examiners would have considered.[37] Two of Blake's early figure drawings

---

37 Bentley assumes that Blake would have been required to submit a large two-foot drawing of an écorché figure with all of the muscles and tendons properly labeled but this is actually not certain. According to Bentley such a drawing was made a formal requirement in 1814, and he believes it would have already been a standard practice when Blake applied for enrollment in 1779, but he gives no proof that this was so. See G. E. Bentley, *Blake Records* (Oxford: Clarendon Press, 1969), 15. In the recent thorough discussion by Anne Wickham of the

clearly drawn from life are both convincingly anatomically correct. For example, in the drawing of the standing figure seen from the side, the shoulder exhibits the relations of the deltoid, the clavicle, the pectoral muscle, and biceps to each other as they occur in the living body. (ill. 16) Most authors suggest that the model for this drawing was Blake's beloved brother Robert. Perhaps this early drawing was made as part of Blake's application for admittance which would account for his observational correctness, or perhaps Blake's attention to the reality of the body of an individual he loved would have stimulated a will to accuracy.

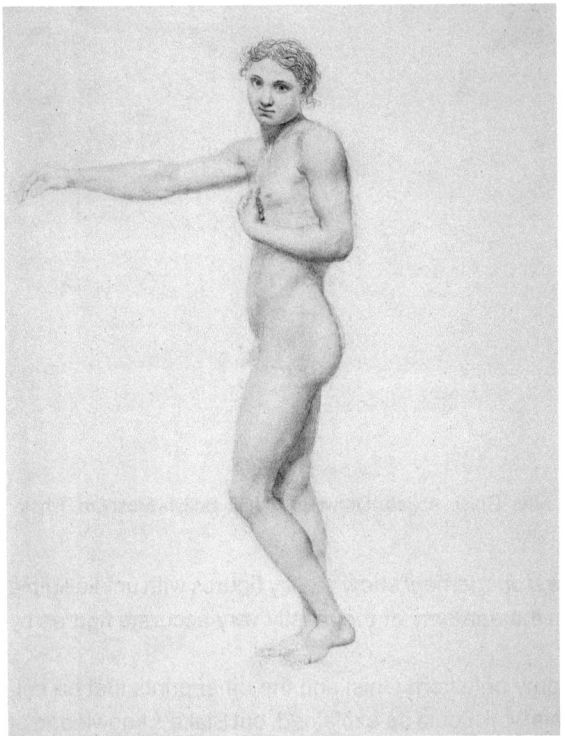

Figure 16. William Blake, *Academic study of a youth, possibly the artist's brother, Robert*, c. 1779–80. Drawing, 479 x 370 cm, British Museum, London. Photo: © British Museum. https://www.britishmuseum.org/collection/object/P_1878-0413-34.

Yet Blake's mature works created after attending the Academy and, presumably, attending Hunter's lectures are unlike the correct anatomy of these two early drawings. Instead, they show that he neither wanted nor needed correct anatomy in his depictions of the body. We see in some of Blake's finest watercolors, for

---

teaching of anatomy at the academy she makes no mention of such a requirement. See Wickham, "Anatomical Studies.", 506–523.

Visionary Anatomy: Blake's Bodies 77

example his illustrations for Robert Blair's poem *The Grave,* case after case of what must be willed deviation from correct depiction of the body. When Blake accepted the commission to illustrate *The Grave* in 1805, he fully expected to also be the engraver of them for a deluxe edition of the poem. To Blake's bitter disappointment, the job of reproducing them for printing was given to the more fashionable engraver Luigi Schiavonetti. Schiavonetti's engravings after Blake have been well known since their publication; Blake's watercolors were lost from view until their rediscovery in a red portfolio on the shelf of a Glasgow bookseller in 2001.[38] Stowed away as they were, these watercolors are beautifully preserved. Schiavonetti faithfully reproduced the poses of the figures and the compositional arrangement from the watercolors, but he also thoroughly altered, indeed corrected, the anatomy of Blake's figures. A comparison of Schiavonetti's engravings to Blake's watercolors – on which they are based – will demonstrate how much Blake diverged from the realities of bone and muscle in the human body and how much Schiavonetti altered Blake's watercolors to depict those realities.

In Blake's watercolor of *The Death of the Strong Wicked Man* (ill. 17), the subject lies on a woven mat that is his death bed. He is in his final agonies while his soul flees out the window. Two clothed women attend the dying man. One stands at his head and covers her face in grief. The other is beside the man in an extreme attitude of excitement that is either grief, fury, or perhaps an unbearable combination of the two. Schiavonetti was a highly skilled artisan, and his engravings capture the emotional power of the watercolors. In his engraving of *The Death of the Strong Wicked Man* (ill. 18) the abdomen of the dying man is contracted as he gasps his final breath. We can plainly see the arch of the lower margin of the rib cage. Where the sternum lies there is an indentation between his pectoral muscles that forms a line which naturally flows into the midline of the belly. In Blake's original watercolor, the margin of the rib cage is not discernible; instead there is a vague structure that is parallel to the lower edge of the pectoral muscle. The line from the sternum tips unnaturally down, creating an impossible hollow in the belly. (This may be more expressive of pain and discomfort than the corresponding area in the engraving, but that is no argument for its correctness.)

The deltoid muscle in Schiavonetti's engraving swells over the shoulder, and we see it emerge from its origin on the clavicle. None of this is clear in the Blake watercolor, and Blake also fails to show distinction between the pectoral and the deltoid muscles. The back of the dying man's soul in the Blake watercolor is a harmonious pattern of subtle relief, but nothing is there that identifiably corresponds to human anatomy. By contrast, the Schiavonetti figure clearly shows the latissimus dorsi inserted into the armpit and the serratus muscle emerging from

---

38 See Nancy Bialler and Robert N. Essick, *William Blake Designs for Blair's Grave* (New York: Sotheby's Inc., 2006).

Figure 17. William Blake, *The Death of the Strong Wicked Man,* 1808. Watercolor, 20.2 x 25.5 cm. Louvre, Paris. Photo: © Louvre Museum/Art Resource.

beneath the lateral edge of the latissimus dorsi. The trapezius muscle is compressed between the shoulder blades and reaches down the back on each side of the vertebra, forming the anatomically correct small triangular gap at the small of the back. The deltoid muscle is correctly inserted between the triceps and the biceps in the engraving, while in Blake's watercolor it seems to go to the other side of the biceps. Furthermore, the thighs of Blake's dying man do not show the diagonal that divides the adductors from the quadriceps which is so clearly visible in the engraving. The division between those two muscle groups is the location of the sartorius muscle which originates at the front top of the pelvis and is inserted into the inner side of the leg at the top of the tibia. Blake's anatomy is rarely correct and also rarely consistent, but the thighs are one part of the body where Blake chooses to be wrong most of the time.

Blake's indifference is indeed so indifferent that he is occasionally correct. One critic asked, "is Blake or is he not interested in muscles? He is not interested enough to get them right."[39] Yet, occasionally, Blake does get muscles right.[40]

---

39 J. R. Harvey, "Blake's Art", 134–5.
40 Two contemporary reviews of the publication of Blake's illustrations are notable in their

Figure 18. Luigi Schiavonetti, *The Death of the Strong Wicked Man*, 1813. Engraving, 280 mm x 248 mm. Metropolitan Museum, New York. Photo: https://www.metmuseum.org/art/collection/search/383668.

Blake rarely diverges from correct anatomy in the arrangement of the two sternomastoid muscles that form the **V** that margins the larynx (ill. 1). An example from the illuminated books is the plate with the two flying fairies blighting the crops which is found in *Europe* (1794). (ill. 19) The muscles on the backs of both figures are patterned with a musculature that only seems convincing at first glance. Analysis shows not only that both figures do not match actual human anatomy, but they do not even match each other, yet the calves of both figures in one version, probably the last, of *Europe* show a simplified but correct display of the gastrocnemius muscles in the calf.[41] Perhaps Blake retreated in this case from

---

different reactions to the incorrectness in Blake's bodies: Robert Hunt wrote that the images are a "futile endeavour by bad drawing to represent immateriality" – an observation made even with Schiavonetti's adjustments to Blake's anatomy. See Bentley, *Blake Records*, 1969, 216. An anonymous reviewer who had seen the original Blake watercolors asked whether "Schiavonetti has done complete justice to the original drawings...the defect of giving strong corporeal semblance to spiritual form was much less glaring in them, than in the prints." (Bentley, 208)

41 All versions of *Europe* can be compared online at the Blake Archive, http://www.blakearchive.org/work/europe.

the deviation from anatomy of these familiar muscles because it would be noticed by his contemporaries: at the turn of the 18th century men wore breeches with their thinly hosed legs observable beneath the knees. It seems that Blake was interested enough in muscles to get them wrong but only in those parts of the body where he believed the incorrectness would not be easily identified by most viewers.

Although Blake's bodies display convexity and overlapping of muscles which make them seem *anatomically convincing*, they actually exhibit subcutaneous bones covered by muscles, insertions, and origins, if discernible, in the wrong place, and non-existent muscles added and important ones omitted, all of which proves his bodies to be *anatomically incorrect.* The bodies cannot achieve their positions by the musculature of which Blake constructs them. The anatomy of Blake's bodies cannot allow them to move in an understandable way, yet they display believable poses and gestures.[42] Blake's figures demonstrate that Hunter's claim that anatomical transgressions destroy the effectiveness of a work of art to be nonsense. By showing actions not caused by the natural laws of the physical world, Blake constructs these actions as miraculous movements of the spirit. In this, Blake's figures seem to embody the lived somatic experience of our own bodies in which we do not discern *how* we move but only *that* we move. The cause that we feel in moving our body is only our will to change position or location. Unless one has studied anatomy one will never think, "I want to raise my arm over my head and so I must contract my deltoid muscle and then follow that contraction by the contraction of the upper portion of my trapezius thus to tilt my scapula away from my rib cage." Though our muscles do exactly these actions, we instead merely think, merely "I want to raise my arm." By not reflecting the how, Blake only shows the fact of movement. By depicting anatomy incorrectly, Blake subverts the logical causality of bodily movement and this is consistent with his rejection extended to the rejection of natural causality in general; the diarist Henry Crabb Robinson reports that in conversation Blake "denied causation, everything being the work of God or Devil."[43] Blake's display of movement without a logical cause is analogous to his assertion which he made to Robinson that the earth is flat.[44] I am sure Blake knew better, but I also believe that he thought the scientific fact of

---

[42] Both Warner and Heppner discuss the meaning of the gestures of Blake's figures as "pathos formulas," a notion that they each derive from Lindberg. My only criticism is the implication that I see in each of these authors that the use of such formulae is in some way particular to Blake. See Janet A. Warner, Blake and the Language of Art (Kingston; Gloucester: McGill-Queen's University Press; A. Sutton, 1984) and Bo Lindberg, William Blake's Illustrations to the Book of Job (Turku, Finland: Abo Akademi, 1973).

[43] Henry Crabb Robinson, "Reminiscences of Blake, 1809–27" in *Lives of William Blake*, ed. Martin Myron (Los Angeles: J. Paul Getty Museum, 2020), 64.

[44] Robinson, "Reminiscences of Blake", 45.

Figure 19. William Blake, *Europe: A Prophecy*, plate 12, copy K, print date 1821. Watercolor on relief etching. pen and ink on paper, 234 x 170 mm. Fitzwilliam Museum, Cambridge. Photo: © Fitzwilliam Museum, Cambridge.

roundness to be irrelevant to how we experience life on the Earth's surface. As he wrote in *Milton*, "every Space that a Man views around his dwelling-place: / Standing on his own roof or in his garden on a mount / Of twenty-five cubits in height, such space is his Universe."[45] I believe that Blake also was aware that living bodies are, in fact, mechanisms that move through a system of joints that are operated by contractions; yet Blake chose to ignore the mechanical relationships between the parts of the body that are necessary for movement because they are as irrelevant to our lived experience as is the shape of our planet.

In rejecting a mechanical understanding of cause and effect in the natural world and in the body in particular, Blake exhibits a consistency with his convictions in a very different realm: his belief in the universal forgiveness of sin. Among the places where Blake expresses his ideas on forgiveness are his emblem book, *The Gates of Paradise* and his late unfinished poem *The Everlasting Gospel*. Forgiveness is the central theme that drives his three great epics, *Milton*, *The Four Zoas*, and *Jerusalem*. For Blake, the notion of punishment for sins is of a piece with the concept of cause and effect and is the negation of the belief in universal forgiveness. Blake sees the idea of a God who is bound to punish the sinful as one where God Himself is trapped in the web of cause and effect. When Milton's God must send his son to atone for the sins of Adam and Eve, it is because God, according to Milton in *Paradise Lost*, Book 3, lacks the freedom to transcend the mechanistic system dictated by an abstract concept of justice. Just as Blake's bodies move as they will without the need for mechanical system of contraction and relaxation, Blake's God can act outside of mechanistic ideas of justice and is free to forgive as God wills. Indeed, Blake's God wills to not punish:

> Listen! Every Religion that Preaches Vengeance for Sins [is] the Religion of the Enemy & Avenger; and not the Forgiver of Sin, and their God is Satan.[46]

Blake sees that a God that does not forgive is neither omnipotent nor merciful and so is hardly God at all.

Blake's anatomical incorrectness, his rejection of causality, and his belief in universal absolute forgiveness of sins are each predicated on his rejection of the mechanistic understanding of the universe. When seen together, they each demonstrate the deep unity of Blake's thought.[47]

All images from the National Gallery of Art, Washington, the Metropolitan Museum of Art, New York, and the Wellcome Collection are in the public domain.

---

45 Blake, Erdman and Bloom, *Complete Poetry and Prose*, 127. *Milton*, Plate 29[31] 5–7.
46 Blake, Erdman and Bloom, *Complete Poetry and Prose*, 201.
47 Thanks to Morris Eaves, Natasha Seaman, and Kevin Salatino for reading this paper and for their valuable suggestions.

Sveinn Yngvi Egilsson
(University of Iceland)

Territorial Kinship and the Feminine Land: Icelandic Patriotic Poetry in an International Context

Abstract
The article compares the Icelandic tradition of patriotic poetry to that of Denmark, from which it took its cue in the eighteenth and nineteenth centuries, and with which it shares some characteristics. Icelandic patriotic poets adopted the central notion of 'territorial kinship', identifying the nation with the land, often through gendered images, especially by personifying the country as a woman or mother. Their poems usually include the following five characteristics: 1. *An address* to the country or the nation; 2. *An enumeration* of the typical characteristics of the country; 3. *The use of common nouns*, as opposed to proper nouns, since the poems are supposed to engage all Icelanders by using general descriptions of their country; 4. *The confirmation of territorial kinship,* i. e. the land as the parent or foster parent of each Icelander; 5. *A wish, a prayer, a blessing or a whetting* on behalf of the country.

Keywords
Patriotic poetry, nationalistic discourse, territorial kinship, symbolic images of nations, Icelandic literature

Patriotic Poems

Patriotic poems can take on various guises, but they are basically a rather standardized kind of poetry.[1] Whether spoken in the singular or the plural, they tend to voice a common cause and often lend themselves to song. As such, they are performative verses, connected with convivial gatherings or celebrations of togetherness and nationality. They are meant to unite a nation and to create a fellow-feeling and solidarity among the people. This is partly achieved through their usual practice of describing the homeland in general rather than specific terms, so that all members of a nation can identify with it, irrespective of their

---

1 For a general description of patriotic poetry, see Joep Leerssen, ed., *Encyclopedia of Romantic Nationalism in Europe*, Vol. I (Amsterdam: Amsterdam University Press, 2018), 109–111.

origins or local attachments. The principal function of patriotic poems – to have the people confirm a kinship with the land – is explained in what follows by putting Icelandic poems of this kind into an international context. This is done with the aim of accounting for the main characteristics of patriotic poems and the nationalistic discourse of which they are part and parcel.[2]

Patriotic poems became prominent in Icelandic literature during the nineteenth century and remained so well into the twentieth century. They played an important part in enhancing patriotic sentiments among Icelanders during their long struggle for self-government, which gathered pace as the nineteenth century wore on.[3] Iceland was part of the Danish kingdom until 1918, when it gained independence from Denmark and finally became an independent republic in 1944. Even though Icelandic patriotic poets were opposed to Denmark as a ruling nation, most of them were educated there, Copenhagen being the capital and the cultural centre of the kingdom. The conventions of Danish patriotic poetry are, therefore, the main point of comparison in this article, because they were the literary model the Icelanders knew, and because Denmark, in general, was the standard against which Icelanders measured themselves and their homeland.

The Icelandic Tradition in a Danish Light

In his 1990 book, *Defining a Nation in Song*, Hans Kuhn researches the reception and the characteristics of Danish patriotic songs by studying songbooks of the period 1832–1870. One of the best-known poems of that tradition is the national song of Denmark, "Der er et yndigt land" (There is a lovely land), written in 1819 by Adam Oehlenschläger (1779–1850). According to Kuhn, this poem lays the groundwork for many patriotic poems which were to follow in Denmark during the nineteenth century. He points out its main characteristics in this context:

(1) the typical physical features of the country
(2) visible reminders of a heroic past
(3) the emotional values of the scenery; its inhabitants

---

2 On the social and convivial functions of patriotic poems in Iceland, as well as their reception and use in poetry collections, student song books, youth clubs, and within the school system, see Sveinn Yngvi Egilsson, *Ísland í Eyjahafinu* (Reykjavík: Hið íslenska bókmenntafélag, 2019), 13–54.
3 For a discussion of Icelandic nationalism, and national identity as expressed in images of nature in patriotic poetry, see Guðmundur Hálfdanarson, *Íslenska þjóðríkið – uppruni og endimörk* (Reykjavík: Hið íslenska bókmenntafélag and ReykjavíkurAkademían, 2007), 191–216. See also Guðmundur Hálfdanarson and Kirsten Thisted, "The Specter of an Empire", in *Denmark and the New North Atlantic: Narratives and Memories in a Former Empire*, Vol. I, ed. Kirsten Thisted and Ann-Sofie N. Gremaud (Aarhus: Aarhus University Press, 2020), 93–177.

(4) the Danes' mental characteristics: language, faith, moral qualities (courage, freedom, loyalty)
(5) Denmark's character within a Scandinavian context
(6) the flag
(7) the sobriety, reliability and honesty particularly found in Jutland
(8) undesirable physical and mental qualities absent from Denmark
(9) culture is blooming in our time
(10) praise of Copenhagen
(11) praise of the present ruler
(12) good wishes, and faith in Denmark's durability.[4]

Kuhn makes the important claim that Oehlenschläger's poem is 'typical of the enumerative approach that was used in many early nineteenth century attempts of this kind, and which echoes the descriptive and didactic genres for which the eighteenth century had such an appetite'.[5] It is furthermore one of many patriotic poems which end in a hopeful way: 'popular songs favour a "conclusion", preferably in a form which draws in the participants, such as a toast in a drinking song. Most patriotic songs have such an element at the end: a pledge, a good wish, a prayer'.[6] According to Kuhn, such poems have a social part to play in a nationalistic sense: 'Patriotic songs function in acts of group communion, even where they say "I" as in "Dengang jeg drog afsted" [when I marched away]'.[7]

Icelandic patriotic poems are characterized by similar features. After *an address* to the country or the nation or to some personification or spirit of the country, the poems go on to *enumerate* the typical characteristics of the country. The enumeration most often consists of *common nouns* (as opposed to proper nouns, place names, etc.) since the poems are supposed to engage all Icelanders by using general rather than particular descriptions of their country. These characteristics can for instance be seen in the poem "Landslag" (Landscape), by Grímur Thomsen:

> Heyrið vella á heiðum hveri, / heyrið álftir syngja í veri: / Íslands er það lag. / Heyrið fljót á flúðum duna, / foss í klettaskorum bruna: / Íslands er það lag.
>
> (Hear the geysers in the highlands! / Hear the swans among the islands! / That is Iceland's song. / Streams through rocky channels sweeping, / Falls through narrow gorges leaping: / That is Iceland's song.)[8]

---

4 Hans Kuhn, *Defining a Nation in Song: Danish Patriotic Songs in Songbooks of the Period 1832–1870* (Copenhagen: C. A. Reitzel, 1990), 124–125.
5 Kuhn, *Defining*, 125.
6 Kuhn, *Defining*, 126.
7 Kuhn, *Defining*, 268.
8 Grímur Thomsen, *Ljóðmæli* (Reykjavík: Mál og menning, 1969), 63; "Iceland's Song. By Grímur Thomsen", translated into English by Jakobína Johnson, *Heimskringla*, 7th issue (7th of November, 1918), 7.

Another example of an address and an enumeration of common nouns (with adjectives) is the poem "Íslands minni" (A Toast to Iceland) by Jónas Hallgrímsson:

> Þið þekkið fold með blíðri brá / og bláum tindi fjalla / og svanahljómi, silungsá / og sælu blómi valla / og bröttum fossi, björtum sjá / og breiðum jökulskalla – / drjúpi' hana blessun drottins á / um daga heimsins alla.
>
> (You know a land with a pleasant countenance / And a blue mountain top / And a song of swan, river of trout / And a happy flower of the fields / And a steep waterfall, a bright sea / And a broad and bare glacier – / May the blessing of the Lord / Pour upon it for the rest of days.)[9]

These concluding lines are in keeping with Kuhn's observation that patriotic poems often end on a note of *blessing, wish,* or *prayer.* While this is true of many Icelandic poems, they can also include a *whetting*, most often directed at Icelanders who were supposed to rally around the cause in the nation's struggle for self-governance. These characteristics will be examined in the following, particularly as found in fifteen poems that were written between the Enlightenment period and the post-war years following the foundation of the republic, and which are among those most often sung and performed in public. One of these poems was written in the eighteenth century, nine in the nineteenth century and five in the twentieth century. They were written by thirteen poets: eleven men and two women (the poems will be cited according to the editions mentioned in the footnotes):

Eggert Ólafsson (1726–1768): "Íslands minni" or 'Ísland ögrum skorið' (A Toast to Iceland or 'Iceland cut with bays') – written in 1757 or earlier.[10]

Bjarni Thorarensen (1786–1841): "Íslands minni" or 'Eldgamla Ísafold' (A Toast to Iceland or 'Ancient Iceland') – written sometime between 1805 and 1811.[11]

Bjarni Thorarensen: "Ísland" or 'Þú nafnkunna landið' (Iceland or 'You renowned land') – written in 1818.[12]

Jónas Hallgrímsson (1807–1845): "Ísland" or 'Ísland! farsældafrón' (Iceland or 'Iceland, fortunate isle') – written in 1835.[13]

---

9 Jónas Hallgrímsson, *Ritverk Jónasar Hallgrímssonar*, Vol. I, *Ljóð og lausamál*, Haukur Hannesson, Páll Valsson and Sveinn Yngvi Egilsson, eds. (Reykjavík: Svart á hvítu, 1989), 108. Literal translations of poetry and prose in this article are by the author, unless otherwise stated.

10 Eggert Ólafsson, *Kvæði* (Copenhagen: S. L. Möller, 1832), 186; cf. Eggert Ólafsson, *Uppkast til forsagna um brúðkaupssiðu hér á landi*, Þorfinnur Skúlason and Örn Hrafnkelsson, eds. (Hafnarfjörður: Söguspekingastifti, 1999), ix, 103.

11 Bjarni Thorarensen, *Ljóðmæli*, Vol. I, Jón Helgason, ed. (Copenhagen: Hið íslenzka fræðafélag, 1935), 27–28.

12 Thorarensen, *Ljóðmæli*, 55–56.

13 Hallgrímsson, *Ritverk*, 63.

Jónas Hallgrímsson: "Íslands minni" or 'Þið þekkið fold með blíðri brá' (A Toast to Iceland or 'You know a land with a pleasant countenance') - written in 1839.[14]

Jón Thoroddsen (1818-1868): "Ó! fögur er vor fósturjörð" ('Oh, fair is our foster earth') - written in 1850.[15]

Bólu-Hjálmar (1796-1875): "Þjóðfundarsöngur 1851" or 'Aldin móðir eðalborna' (Song for the National Assembly 1851 or 'Old and noble mother') - written in 1851.[16]

Steingrímur Thorsteinsson (1831-1913): "Vorhvöt" or 'Þú, vorgyðja! svífur úr suðrænum geim' (Spring Cry or 'Goddess of spring! you glide from a southern sphere') - written in 1870.[17]

Matthías Jochumsson (1835-1920): "Lofsöngur" or 'Ó, Guð vors lands!' (Song of Praise or 'Oh, God of our land!') - written in 1873-1874.[18]

Grímur Thomsen (1820-1896): "Landslag" or 'Heyrið vella á heiðum hveri' (Landscape or 'Hear the geysers in the highlands') - written in 1875.[19]

Stephan G. Stephansson (1853-1927): "Úr Íslendingadags ræðu" or 'Þó þú langförull legðir' (From a speech on Icelander's day or 'Though you travelled wide and far') - written in 1904.[20]

Hulda (Unnur Benediktsdóttir Bjarklind, 1881-1946): "Hver á sér fegra föðurland" ('Who has a fairer fatherland') - written in 1944.[21]

Jóhannes úr Kötlum (1899-1972): "Íslendingaljóð 17. júní 1944" or 'Land míns föður' (A poem of Icelanders 17th June 1944 or 'Land of my father') - written in 1944.[22]

Guðmundur Böðvarsson (1904-1974): "Fylgd" or 'Komdu, litli ljúfur' (Escort or 'Come, sweet little one') - written in 1948.[23]

Margrét Jónsdóttir (1893-1971): "Ísland er land þitt" ('Iceland is your land') - written in 1954.[24]

All of these poems are patriotic in that they voice the common connection with the homeland, but they also show the variety of tone or mode within the tradition. Some are rather earthbound in their praise, such as Ólafsson's "Íslands minni" ('Ísland ögrum skorið'), Thorarensen's "Íslands minni" ('Eldgamla Ísafold') and

---

14 Hallgrímsson, Ritverk, 108.
15 Jón Thoroddsen, Kvæði (Copenhagen: Sigurður Kristjánsson, 1919), 1-2. The poem was published in the novel Piltur og stúlka (Boy and girl) in 1850.
16 Hjálmar Jónsson frá Bólu, Ljóðmæli, Vol. I, Finnur Sigmundsson, ed. (Reykjavík: Ísafoldarprentsmiðja, 1949), 5-6.
17 Steingrímur Thorsteinsson, Ljóðmæli: Heildarútgáfa frumsaminna ljóða (Reykjavík: Prentsmiðjan Leiftur, 1958), 106-108.
18 Matthías Jochumsson, Ljóð: Úrval, Ólafur Briem, ed. (Reykjavík: Rannsóknastofnun í bókmenntafræði and Menningarsjóður, 1980), 99-100.
19 Grímur Thomsen, Ljóðmæli, 63.
20 Stephan G. Stephansson, Andvökur, Sigurður Nordal, ed. (Reykjavík: Mál og menning, 1980), 113-114.
21 Kristinn E. Andrésson, ed., Svo frjáls vertu móðir: Nokkur ættjarðarljóð 1944-1954 (Reykjavík: Mál og menning, 1954), 20-21.
22 Andrésson, Svo frjáls vertu móðir, 22-23.
23 Andrésson, Svo frjáls vertu móðir, 37-39.
24 Margrét Jónsdóttir, Ný ljóð (Reykjavík: Barnablaðið Æskan, 1970), 7-8.

Hulda's "Hver á sér fegra föðurland", all of which have been held in high regard by the Icelandic people and served as informal national anthems over the course of time. Others are grandiose and soaring, such as "Lofsöngur" (Song of Praise) by reverend Matthías Jochumsson, which is in fact a variation on a theme from Psalm 90 in the Old Testament and written in 1874 for the celebration of the millennium of Iceland's settlement.[25] This song has been established by tradition as the national anthem of Iceland since the early twentieth century.[26] It was formally declared so in 1983, when the Icelandic parliament passed Act no. 7/1983, under which law no one may perform or publish the national anthem in any other form than the original. Asking for the blessing of God and mixing the religious with the patriotic is a well-known practice in nationalism and patriotic poetry throughout the world, as for instance in the Commonwealth anthem "God Save the Queen" and Denmark's "Bøn for Danmark or Kongernes Konge! ene Du kan / Skjærme vort elskede Fædreland!" (Prayer for Denmark or King of Kings! only you / Can shield our beloved fatherland!). Written in 1848 by Adolph Recke (1820-1867), the latter was a kind of call to arms in the Schleswig-Holstein War. Its militant tone is common to many patriotic poems, as in "God Save the Queen", in which God is asked to scatter the enemies of the sovereign and make them fall. Even in Jochumsson's religious and hymn-like praise, God is addressed as a 'hertogi' (duke or warlord) with his 'herskari' (heavenly host or army).[27] Recke addresses God in this way (second stanza):

> Slyng om os Alle Enigheds Baand!
> Send fra din Himmel Begeistringens Aand!
> > Følg Du i Fare
> > Den tappre, lille Skare!
> Løft over Hæren din velsignende Haand![28]
>
> (Wrap around us all the band of unity!
> Send from your heaven the spirit of enthusiasm!
> > Follow in danger

---

25 Gunnlaugur A. Jónsson, "Íslands þúsund ár: Sálmur 90 í sögu og samtíð", *Ritröð Guðfræðistofnunar* 15 (2001), 52-55.
26 Steingrímur J. Þorsteinsson, "Formáli", in *Ó, guð vors lands: Þjóðsöngur Íslendinga* (Reykjavík: Forsætisráðuneytið, 1957), 6.
27 In the 19th century, the word *hertogi* was used in a more military sense than today, when it simply refers to royalty or nobility. For instance, when Jochumsson's periodical *Þjóðólfur* (32nd year, 6th issue, 1880, 22) quotes an obituary about Jón Sigurðsson, the recently deceased leader of the Icelandic struggle for self-government, he is described in this way: 'hann var hertogi í þeirri orrustu fyrir frelsi og forræði, sem meir en heilan mannsaldur hefir þegar verið háð á Íslandi á móti hinni skrifstofulegu stjórn hér suður í Danmörku' (he was a warlord in that fight for freedom and sovereignty, which for more than a generation has already been fought in Iceland against the bureaucratic government south here in Denmark).
28 Kuhn, *Defining*, 222.

The brave, little crowd!
Raise over the army your blessing hand!)

Throughout the nineteenth century, Thorarensen's "Íslands minni" ('Eldgamla Ísafold') had served as an informal national anthem. Most often sung to the same tune as the Commonwealth anthem, it may originally have been composed to another tune by Édouard Du Puy.[29] "Íslands minni" was first printed in a 1819 multilingual student songbook entitled *Studenterviser, i dansk, islandsk, latinsk og græsk Maal*, and it quickly grew in popularity.[30] A year later (1820) it was given, along with "God Save the King our King!", as the tune to the poem "Þjóðsöngur Hjálmars á Bjargi" (The National Anthem of Hjálmar at Bjarg) by Magnús Stephensen (1762-1833).[31] Those who gather in Þingvellir, the old assembly site in Iceland, in a fictional account in the periodical *Ármann á alþingi* (1829), sing Thorarensen's poem and make a toast to the nation and the land.[32] This shows how "Íslands minni" gradually achieved the status of an informal national anthem, even though its poetical merits were still open to debate.[33]

In his preface to *Sýnisbók íslenzkra bókmennta á 19. öld* (An Antology of Icelandic Literature in the nineteenth Century), Bogi Th. Melsteð (1860-1929) made the claim that Thorarensen's poem was a turning point in Icelandic literature: 'Þjóðsöngurinn Eldgamla Ísafold hefur líka þýðingu í skáldskap vorum sem kvæði Oehlenschlägers um gullhornin í hinum danska; hvorttveggja boðar nýjan tíma' (The national anthem Eldgamla Ísafold has a similar standing in our literature to Oehlenschläger's poem on the golden horns in Danish literature; both are heralds of a new age).[34] The poem "Guldhornene" (The golden horns) by Adam Oehlenschläger (written in 1802) was generally accepted to mark the beginning of the romantic movement in Denmark, and it is clear that Melsteð attaches an equal importance to "Íslands minni". The Austrian author and translator J. C. Poestion (1853-1922) confirmed his claim when he said that

---

29 Cf. Jón Helgason's comment in Bjarni Thorarensen, *Ljóðmæli*, Vol. II (Copenhagen: Hið íslenzka fræðafélag, 1935), 41.
30 *Studenterviser, i dansk, islandsk, latinsk og græsk Maal. Med Bidrag af Prof. Oehlenschläger, Prof. Finn Magnussen, Pastor Michelsen og Andre; samt med Musik af Prof. Weyse og fl.*, Semper Hilaris [Sylvester Herz], ed. (Copenhagen: A. Seidelin, 1819), 119-120.
31 Magnús Stephensen, *Ræður Hjálmars á Bjargi fyrir Børnum sínum um Fremd, kosti og annmarka allra Stétta, og um þeirra almennustu Gjöld og Tekjur* (Viðeyjarklaustur: Magnús Stephensen, 1820), 147. This is in fact the oldest occurrence of the word *þjóðsöngur* in print but it also occurs in the periodicals *Skírnir* (1828, 32) and *Fjölnir* (1838, II, 15).
32 *Ármann á Alþíngi*, 1st year, 1829, 210-212.
33 For a detailed discussion of the age, text, and social environment of the poem, see Þórir Óskarsson, "Eldgamla Ísafold: Aldur, texti og félagslegt umhverfi", *Andvari*, 147th year, 2022, 83-103.
34 Bogi Th. Melsteð, "Formáli", in *Sýnisbók íslenzkra bókmennta á 19. öld* (Copenhagen: Gyldendal, 1891), vi.

Thorarensen's poem 'für die isländische Poesie eine ähnliche Bedeutung erlangte wie Oehlenschlägers Dichtung für die dänische' (had gained a similar importance for the Icelandic poetry as Oehlenschläger's poetry for the Danish).[35] Poet and scholar Benedikt Gröndal (1826-1907) disagreed, however, observing that "Íslands minni" was 'ekkert sjerlega skáldlegt kvæði, og það hefir orðið þjóðsöngur af vana, en ekki af öðru' (not a very accomplished poem, and it has become a national anthem out of habit, but not because of anything else).[36]

Despite such criticisms, Thorarensen's "Íslands minni" struck a chord that resounded in many Icelandic patriotic poems during the nineteenth and twentieth centuries. The female personification of Iceland had in fact been introduced earlier, in poems and visual depictions by the Enlightenment author and naturalist Eggert Ólafsson, but Thorarensen gave her the name *fjallkona* (Mountain Woman), which stuck and has since been used both in poetry and general parlance.[37] In his "Íslands minni" ('Ísland ögrum skorið'), Ólafsson imagined the land as a mother or foster mother, 'sem á brjóstum borið / og blessað hefir mig / fyrir skikkun skaparans, / vertu blessað, blessi þig / blessað nafnið hans' (Who has held in her bosom / And blessed me / As God has arranged, / May you be blessed, and bless you / His blessed name). This image of the blessed and blessing motherland or native land corresponds to Ólafsson's comments in another text of his, that everybody should feel obliged 'að elska og rækja [landið] af öllum kröftum ei einasta vegna þess það hefur fætt og fóstrað oss; heldur og hins að sá er Guðs vilji og forsjón' (to love and cultivate [the land] with all one's might not only because it has fed and fostered us; but also because such is God's will and providence).[38] The speaker in Thorarensen's poem also talks as one of the sons of the motherly land: 'Fjallkonan fríð! / mögum þín muntu kær, / meðan lönd gyrðir sær' (Fair Mountain Woman! / You will be dear to your sons, / As long as the sea surrounds the lands). In this way, Thorarensen passed on the female personification of Iceland from the Enlightenment poetry of the eighteenth century to romanticism in the nineteenth century and beyond. The Mountain Woman has

---

35 J. C. Poestion, *Isländische Dichter der Neuzeit in Charakteristiken und übersetzten Proben ihrer Dichtung* (Leipzig: Verlag von Georg Heinrich Meyer, 1897), 294.
36 Benedikt Gröndal, "Nokkur orð um íslenzkar bækur og rit. II. (Síðari greinin)", *Ísafold* (18th year, 81st issue, 10th of October, 1891), 319.
37 Þórkatla Óskarsdóttir Helgason, *Ideas of Nationality in Icelandic Poetry 1830-1874*, Ph.D. dissertation (Edinburgh: University of Edinburgh, 1982), 72, 82; Þórunn Valdimarsdóttir, "Um gagnkvæma ást manna og meyjar (fjallkonunnar)", in *Yrkja: Afmælisrit til Vigdísar Finnbogadóttur*, Heimir Pálsson et. al., eds. (Reykjavík: Iðunn, 1990), 290-291; Hallfreður Örn Eiríksson, "Hugmyndir íslenskra höfunda á 19. öld um þjóðarbókmenntir: Nokkrir þættir", in *Sagnaþing helgað Jónasi Kristjánssyni sjötugum*, Gísli Sigurðsson, Guðrún Kvaran and Sigurgeir Steingrímsson, eds. (Reykjavík: Hið íslenska bókmenntafélag, 1994), 352-354.
38 Eggert Ólafsson, *Uppkast til forsagna*, 100.

proven to be a long-lived image in nationalistic discourse in Iceland and festive occasions of many kinds (more on which below).[39]

Thorarensen's poem also takes issue with Denmark and especially with Copenhagen as a place of dissipation and decadence. On behalf of Icelanders living in this unhealthy city who wish to be back home in Iceland, the speaker says: 'Hafnar úr gufu hér / heim allir girnumst vér' (From the vapour here / We long for home). They have lost their way and fallen prey to the temptations of city life, so that 'hlær að oss heimskinginn / Hafnar-slóð á' (We are laughed at by the fool / In Copenhagen). The poem derides Denmark as a face without a nose, negatively contrasting its flatness to mountainous and well-proportioned Iceland in the North. This kind of comparison is common to many patriotic poems, in which the homeland is held to be superior to other countries, especially when one of the latter is also a source of subjugation. In Scandinavian poetry, the flatness of Denmark had been contrasted to the mountains of Norway since the eighteenth century.[40] The particularity of Iceland has long inflected Icelandic patriotic poems and nationalistic discourse. Even a poem as tranquil as Hulda's "Hver á sér fegra föðurland" (Who has a fairer fatherland), written during the Second World War, has a certain sharpness. The speaker points out that Iceland is far removed from 'heimsins vígaslóð' (the battlefield of the world) but asks at the same time for the nation never to be 'öðrum þjóðum háð' (dependent on other nations). Iceland's long struggle for self-government still resonated in 1944, when poets like Hulda celebrated the foundation of a republic in Iceland. The danger of becoming dependent on other nations was of course easily felt because of the war, and also because Iceland was, at that time, under U.S. military occupation.

Thorarensen's second poem, "Ísland" or 'Þú nafnkunna landið' ("Iceland" or 'You renowned land'), presents Iceland's natural forces and local conditions as fortifying elements of geographic determinism. 'Undarlegt sambland af frosti og funa' (A strange mixture of frost and fire) are natural conditions that can harden the Icelandic people and enhance their character. In contrast to the gentle south, the harsher nature and colder climate of the north helps to build character, health, and prowess. Thus, the northerly position of Iceland, its isolation in the middle of the North Atlantic, the landscape of the country, its many mountains, even the frequent volcanic eruptions, as well as the climate itself, the snow and frost, are all part of a character-building process, from which the nation could

---

39 Árni Björnsson, *Saga daganna* (Reykjavík: Mál og menning, 1993), 152–154; Terry Gunnell, "The Development and Role of the *Fjallkona* (Mountain Woman) in Icelandic National Day Celebrations and Other Contexts", in *The Ritual Year 11: Traditions and Transformation*, Guzel Stolyarova, Irina Sedakova and Nina Vlaskina, eds. (Kazan and Moskva: T8, 2016), 22–40.
40 Kuhn, *Defining*, 244.

benefit greatly.[41] It is necessary, however, for the nation to be equal to this invigorating challenge. Icelanders should at all costs avoid 'vellyst' (sensuality) and 'læpuskaps ódyggðir' (the vices of faint-heartedness) which could enter the country from abroad. In the case of some external danger, the land and the Icelandic climate are to be the guardians of national virtues:

> Þó vellyst í skipsförmum völskunum meður
> vafri að landi, eg skaða ei tel;
> því útfyrir kaupstaði íslenzkt í veður
> ef hún sér vogar, þá frýs hún í hel.

> (Even if sensuality as a cargo in ships, along with the rats,
> Wanders ashore, I count it not as a loss;
> Because if it dares to go outside the towns
> Into the Icelandic weather, it freezes to death.)

The sublime beauty of the homeland should also encourage the people to revive their former glory, as suggested in the poem "Ísland" ('Ísland! farsældafrón') by Jónas Hallgrímsson. As Hallgrímsson suggests, despite a reversal of fortune during the preceding centuries, as compared to the golden age of Iceland's medieval period, the land is still 'fagurt og frítt og fannhvítir jöklanna tindar' (fair and beautiful and the peaks of the glaciers white as snow). The poem is an example of the complicated relationship Icelandic poets had with national romanticism in Denmark. Hallgrímsson wrote it in 1835, applying the elegiac metre which originated in Ancient Greece, but which had hardly been used in Icelandic poetry up to that point. This metre had, however, been previously used by Adam Oehlenschläger, Denmark's 'national poet', in a poem on the medieval glory of Iceland ("Island" or 'Island, hellige Ø', published in 1805, revised in 1823 as 'Island, Oldtidens Ø').[42] It seems quite obvious that Hallgrímsson based his poem on Oehlenschläger's example, which showed how age-honoured metres could be used to nationalistic ends, promoting a glorious image of the past in order to revive it in the present. But receiving this model from the poetical representative of the ruling nation was by no means unproblematic for an emerging poet of the subordinate nation. It is yet another example of Icelandic patriotic poets learning

---

41 Bjarni Guðnason, "Bjarni Thorarensen og Montesquieu", in *Afmælisrit Jóns Helgasonar*, eds. Jakob Benediktsson, Jón Samsonarson, Jónas Kristjánsson, Ólafur Halldórsson and Stefán Karlsson (Reykjavík: Heimskringla, 1969), 34–47; Sveinn Yngvi Egilsson, "The sublime North: Iceland as an artistic discourse originating in the nineteenth century", in *Exploring NORDIC COOL in Literary History*, eds. Gunilla Hermansson and Jens Lohfert Jørgensen (Amsterdam: John Benjamins Publishing, 2020), 191–204, esp. 192–194.

42 Sveinn Yngvi Egilsson, *Náttúra ljóðsins: Umhverfi íslenskra skálda* (Reykjavík: Bókmennta- og listfræðastofnun Háskóla Íslands, 2014), 58; cf. Sveinn Yngvi Egilsson, *Arfur og umbylting: Rannsókn á íslenskri rómantík* (Reykjavík: Hið íslenska bókmenntafélag and Reykjavíkur- Akademían, 1999), 342–346.

the trade from the poets of the nation they were really writing against, in their struggle for independence. Both poems have all the main characteristics of patriotic poetry, including an address and an enumeration, but they are uncharacteristic in using proper nouns instead of common nouns, listing names known from medieval sources (Oehlenschläger mentions some of the Old Norse gods, heroes, and poets; Hallgrímsson mentions a few saga heroes and chieftains in connection with the annual assembly in Þingvellir).

Oehlenschläger describes Iceland as a place of memories: 'Ihukommelsens vældigste Tempel' (Memory's mightiest temple). The poem's triumphant climax reimagines the great sculptor Bertel Thorvaldsen (1770–1844; a Dane of Icelandic descent) as a hammer-wielding, modern-day Thor, rejuvenating the past: '*Thor fra Island i Rom vækker Kronion til Liv!*' (*Thor from Iceland in Rome brings Kronion to life!*).[43] Hallgrímsson uses the glorious image of medieval Iceland much more provocatively. After describing the Icelandic Commonwealth and the assembly in Þingvellir in vivid detail, he ends his poem with a general rebuke that amounts to a whetting: 'Ó, þér unglingafjöld og Íslands fullorðnu synir! / Svona er feðranna frægð fallin í gleymsku og dá!' (Oh, you multitude of youngsters and grown-up sons of Iceland! / This is how the fame of the fathers has fallen into forgetfulness and oblivion!). Earlier in the poem he had described Iceland as a 'farsælda frón og hagsælda hrímhvíta móðir' (fortunate isle and prosperity's hoar-frosted mother). The 'sons' in the poem are reminded of their obligation to their common 'mother', the land, just as Hallgrímsson's predecessors, Eggert Ólafsson and Bjarni Thorarensen, had emphasized similar patriotic sentiments in their works. Nationalistic discourse often becomes ethical in this sense, through the preaching of patriotic virtues regarding the obligation of each Icelander towards the native land, and the necessity of opposing foreign forces and influences, especially the ruling nation. These are well-known manifestations of nationalism in an international context. They can be better understood in view of certain key concepts which theorists in nationalistic studies have applied when explaining the special relationship between a nation and its homeland.

Territorial Kinship

The Icelandic patriotic poems under investigation all include a description of the land and, at the same time, refer to the history of the nation, either directly or indirectly. As Kuhn explains, these two factors – the land or landscape and the national history – are common themes: 'Landscape and history are, at least in the

---

43 Adam Oehlenschläger, "Island", *Poetiske Skrifter* I (Copenhagen: J. H. Schubothe, 1805), 233, 236.

19th century, the two main pillars of patriotic poetry'.[44] Icelandic poets sometimes use shorthand to refer to the history of the nation, as Matthías Jochumsson does in his line 'Íslands þúsund ár' (Iceland's thousand years), which is a quick reminder of the span of Icelandic history from 874 to 1874, or from the settlement era to the time of writing. Other poets cover periods of Icelandic history in greater detail, an example of which we have already seen in the Commonwealth description by Jónas Hallgrímsson in his poem "Ísland".

In a book chapter on Icelandic patriotic poems, the scholar Guðrún Nordal describes the historical connection of the nation and the land in this way:

> Í orðinu ættjarðarljóð felst vísbending um myndmál þessara kvæða. Fólk rekur *ætt* sína til þeirrar veru sem fóstraði það. Í öllum ættjarðarljóðum verður vart spennu milli mannfólks og náttúru, frjáls náttúran hvetur ánauðugan Íslending til dáða, sveitirnar minna hann á liðna sögu, horfna gullöld. Eitt lífseigasta táknið fyrir ættjörðina er konan; móðirin sem varðveitir barn sitt í skauti sér eða fjallkonan sem situr eins og fjarlæg drottning, einhvers konar huldukona í hásæti sínu, búin skautbúningi fjallanna. Tvær upphafnar kvenmyndir skáldanna, sem nær öll eru karlar.
>
> (The word ættjarðarljóð [kin-earth poem] suggests the imagery of these poems. People trace their lineage to the being that fostered them. In all patriotic poems there is a tension between humans and nature; free nature encourages the oppressed Icelander, the countryside reminds him of a history that has passed, a golden age that is gone. One of the most persistent symbols for the ættjörð [kin-earth] is the woman; the mother who guards her child in her lap or the mountain woman who sits like a distant queen, some kind of elf woman on her throne, dressed in the festive national costume of the mountains. Two exalted images of women by poets, who are almost all men.)[45]

Describing the native land as one's *parent* or *foster parent* is a key factor in nationalistic discourse. Icelandic words like *móðurjörð*, *föðurland* and *fósturjörð* (mother earth, fatherland and foster earth) are comparable to words like *Vaterland* in German, *motherland* in English, *fædreland* in Danish and *fosterjord* in Swedish. Such words are found throughout European languages and are manifestations of what has been defined as *territorial kinship*,[46] which can also include the notion of land as the native *home*, as in the German *Heimat*, the Danish *hjemland* and the English *homeland*. Whether the land is identified with kinship,

---

44 Kuhn, *Defining*, 212.
45 Guðrún Nordal, "Landið", in *Skiptidagar: Nesti handa nýrri kynslóð* (Reykjavík: Mál og menning, 2018), 108.
46 Steven Grosby, "Time, Kinship, and the Nation", in *Genealogy* 2/2 (2018), 17: https://www.mdpi.com/2313-5778/2/2/17/htm; Steven Grosby, *Nationalism: A Very Short Introduction* (Oxford: Oxford University Press, 2005), 43–56. See also Anthony D. Smith, *Nationalism and Modernism: A Critical Survey of Recent Theories of Nations and Nationalism* (London and New York: Routledge, 1998), 145–169, and Anthony D. Smith, *Ethno-Symbolism and Nationalism: A Cultural Approach* (London and New York: Routledge, 2009), 8–9, 47–48, 112–113.

parenting, or a home, the associated imagery or metaphor is used to suggest that one feels close to the land.

What familial descent and nationality have in common is that neither is optional but decided by birth. All who are born descend from certain individuals and belong to a group of natives.[47] This involves a similar sense of obligation to one's family and nation. Furthermore, nationality is bound to a certain area or land, as nations identify themselves with such territories, and with earlier generations who settled and cultivated these territories before them. In nationalistic and patriarchal discourse these predecessors are often seen as *founding fathers* in a kind of *origin myth*.[48] In patriotic literature they find their expression in *foundational epics* that involve the rewriting or reinterpretation of old sources.[49] Hallgrímsson bases his poem "Ísland" on such an origin myth, describing the Norwegian settlers of Iceland as freedom-loving founding fathers:

> Þá komu feðurnir frægu og frjálsræðishetjurnar góðu
> austan um hyldýpishaf, hingað í sælunnar reit.
> Reistu sér byggðir og bú í blómguðu dalanna skauti ...
>
> (Then came the famous fathers and the good heroes of freedom
> From the east across the deep sea, to this area of happiness.
> Built themselves settlements and farms in the blooming bosom of the valleys ...).

Predecessors in patriotic poems, however, are not exclusively imagined as belonging to a distant and mythical past. They can also be a closer and clearer presence in the poems, as is the case with the father in "Land míns föður" (My father's land), by Jóhannes úr Kötlum, and with the father who addresses his son in Guðmundur Böðvarsson's poem "Fylgd" (Escort), encouraging him to care for the land. Patriotic poets like Jón Thoroddsen remind their fellow Icelanders that Earth keeps the physical remains of the predecessors: 'Þú fósturjörðin fríð og kær, / sem feðra hlúar beinum' (You fair and dear foster earth, / Who nurses the bones of fathers). Descriptions of the close connection of the nation with the land are therefore not necessarily far-fetched or metaphorical but may be based on the simple fact that Earth accommodates both the living and the dead. This is put memorably in the "Prologue" to the thirteenth-century scholarly work, *Snorra-Edda* (*The Prose Edda*), which describes the Earth in this way: 'hon fæddi ǫll kykvendi ok hon eignaðiz alt þat, er dó; fyrir þá sǫk gáfu þeir henni nafn ok tǫlðu

---

47 Benedict Anderson, *Imagined Communities: Reflections on the Origin and Spread of Nationalism*, a printing of the revised edition from 2006 (first edition, 1983) (London and New York: Verso, 2016), 143–144.
48 Smith, *Nationalism and Modernism*, 62–63, 115, and *Ethno-Symbolism and Nationalism*, 27–28, 47–48, 91–92.
49 Anne-Marie Thiesse, *The Creation of National Identities: Europe, 18th–20th Centuries* (National Cultivation of Culture, Vol. 26, Leiden, Boston: Brill, 2021), 84–99.

ætt sína til hennar' (she nourished all creatures and she took to her everything that died; for that reason they gave her a name and traced their lineage to her).[50] Medieval people, just like latter-day patriotic poets, had a clear understanding of the essential part the Earth plays in the life of each and every creature. The fertile Earth is acknowledged as a provider of life in the Icelandic poems. Patriotic imagery can become organic or floral in such instances, where the soil itself is shown to provide and nurture the life of the nation. Examples of this are Bjarni Thorarensen's 'ástkær fósturmold' (Beloved foster soil), Matthías Jochumsson's 'Ó, Guð vors lands! ó, lands vors Guð! / vér lifum sem blaktandi, blaktandi strá' (Oh, God of our land! oh, our land's God! / We live as a fluttering, fluttering straw), and Margrét Jónsdóttir's 'íslenzka moldin, er lífið þér gaf' (The Icelandic soil, which gave you your life).

The concept of territorial kinship is applicable not only to the connection with the land discussed above, but also to the historical rights and duties of those who have lived in the land and lay claim to it.[51] The sense of duty weighs heavily in this context, especially the perceived patriotic obligation to care for the native land, which is also seen as an extension of duty to family or predecessors. This twofold duty is included in the word *ættjörð*, where the *ætt* [kin] and the Earth are combined, as Guðrún Nordal points out. Duty is often defined in patriarchal terms as owed to the forefathers who settled, cultivated, and laid their claim to the land, as is evident in the common word *föðurland* (Eng. *fatherland*, Ger. *Vaterland*). In Icelandic poetry and parlance, however, this duty is more often connected to the image of the country as a woman. The feminine personification of Iceland is part of a larger trend during the upsurge of European nationalism in the eighteenth and nineteenth centuries, when various countries used such allegorical images of women to define themselves and their perceived national virtues. Even if they are only symbolic, these feminine personifications merit further inspection.

The Feminine Land

In patriotic poetry, the feminine personification of Iceland is most often magnificent, showing the country in the guise of a glorious and empowered woman in beautiful attire. Various Icelandic poems of the eighteenth and nineteenth centuries, however, offer an alternative and contrasting image of the country. In the mid-eighteenth century, Enlightenment poet Eggert Ólafsson presented Iceland as an old and suffering woman, 'í líkingu einnar konu' (in the likeness of a woman)

---

50 *Edda Snorra Sturlusonar*, Finnur Jónsson, ed. (Copenhagen: Gyldendal, 1931), 2.
51 Grosby, "Time, Kinship, and the Nation", and *Nationalism*, 51-56.

who is 'sorg og elli mædd' (beset with sorrow and old age).[52] He also personified the Icelandic language in a similar way: "Sótt og dauði Íslenskunnar, hinnar afgömlu móður vorrar; í tveimur kvæðum framsett" (The illness and death of Icelandic, our ancient mother; presented in two poems).[53] In a preamble to yet another poem, he imagined Iceland as a woman who 'hefir yfir sér svarta kvenskikkju þrönga ... þessi kona hefir með öllu sorgliga ásýnd' (is dressed in a black, close-cut lady's cloak ... this woman has a wholly sorrowful countenance).[54] These sad and sorry images of Iceland and the Icelandic language were supposed to reflect their precarious condition in the eighteenth century. Ólafsson felt that the national culture and the language itself were in danger, owing not only to unfortunate circumstances, but also to the lethargy of the Icelandic people. The sorrowful and forlorn personifications are a form of whetting, as they are meant to urge the Icelanders to do something about the sorry state of their land and language.

The image of Iceland as an old and sad woman continued into the nineteenth century and was used as a kind of whetting in politically engaged poetry. A case in point is "Þjóðfundarsöngur 1851" (Song for the National Assembly 1851) by Hjálmar Jónsson, in which Iceland is depicted as an old mother – 'Aldin móðir eðalborna, / Ísland' (Old and noble mother, / Iceland) – who is grotesquely bloodmilked: 'Þér á brjósti barn þitt liggur, / blóðfjaðrirnar sogið fær' (Your child lies at your breast, / Gets to suck the blood [since the milk has run out]). The poet worried about the fate of his nation and wanted to whet the Icelandic representatives at the National Assembly in 1851, where the political status of Iceland was to be decided. As it turned out, Count Trampe (1807–1868), the Danish governor of Iceland, presented a bill to the assembly which would have made the Danish constitution of 1849 valid in Iceland. This bill was rejected in the assembly, as the Icelanders felt that their country would simply become a rural commune within the Danish state. Instead, they proposed a constitution for an independent Iceland in personal union with the Danish king. Count Trampe found this unacceptable and dissolved the meeting, to which the Icelanders objected and, under the leadership of Jón Sigurðsson (1811–1879), shouted in unison: 'Vér mótmælum allir!' (We all protest!). While this led to an impasse in the matter, it proved, in the long run, to be consequential for the Icelanders' struggle for self-government, eventually resulting in the Constitution of Iceland in 1874.[55]

---

52 Ólafsson, Kvæði, 9.
53 Ólafsson, Kvæði, 124–132.
54 Ólafsson, Kvæði, 107–108.
55 Aðalgeir Kristjánsson, Endurreisn alþingis og þjóðfundurinn (Reykjavík: Sögufélag, 1993), 305–333; Gunnar Karlsson, "Upphafsskeið þjóðríkismyndunar 1830–1874", in Saga Íslands, Vol. IX, ed. Sigurður Líndal and Pétur Hrafn Árnason (Reykjavík: Hið íslenzka bókmenntafélag and Sögufélag, 2008), 271–279; Guðmundur Hálfdanarson, "Severing the Ties – Ice-

Ill. 1: An allegorical depiction, entitled *A Painting of the Icelandic Language, 1766, and Its Explanation in the Mother Tongue*, based on the ideas of Eggert Ólafsson. The dark-clad woman in the centre represents Icelandic, who has the female personifications of Poverty and Gratitude on either side. The engraving was made in 1766, celebrating the new king on the Danish throne, Christian VII (bust on the right), while paying a sorrowful tribute to his father, the newly deceased Frederick V (the urn and crying infant on the left). The land itself is covered with snow, as the king died in the depth of winter, but the accompanying text also emphasizes how poverty has held Iceland in its grip, while the stork is said to symbolize cultivation and love.

In his "Þjóðfundarsöngur 1851", Hjálmar Jónsson reminds his fellow countrymen of their obligation towards the native land and their shared history. He even suggests that the nation has failed in this respect, as he threatens those who will not come to the rescue of their country, still personifying it as an ageing mother:

land's Journey from a Union with Denmark to a Nation-State", *Scandinavian Journal of History* 31 (2006), 237–254.

Móðir vor með fald og feldi
fannhvítum á kroppi sér,
hnigin að æfi kalda kveldi,
karlæg nær og holdlaus er;
grípi hver sitt gjald í eldi,
sem gengur frá að bjarga þér.

(Our mother with high headdress
And snow-white fur on her body,
Advanced into the cold night of life,
Almost bedridden and flesh-less;
Those who will refrain from saving you
May find their punishment in fire.)

The sad image of Mother Iceland was used by other poets as well, to stir their countrymen up in the national cause. Steingrímur Thorsteinsson, a close collaborator of Jón Sigurðsson and one of the chief poets of the Icelandic movement for independence, did this for instance in his poem "Vorhvöt" (Spring Cry): 'Vér heitum þann níðing sem hæðir þín tár / og hendur á móður vill binda' (We call him a villain who mocks your tears / And wants to tie the hands of mother). Similar images of sad or tragic female personifications are known from other nations such as Poland, where *Polonia* (the Polish Mother) became a tragic figure in literature and art. She was often shown in mourning attire, reflecting the ordeals of the Polish people during the nineteenth century.[56]

The contrasting image of the glorious Mountain Woman (*fjallkona*) represents the ideal of Icelandic empowerment and sovereignty. Steingrímur Thorsteinsson also calls her *eykona* (Island Woman) in his poem "Ísland", as does Jón Thoroddsen in his poem "Til Íslendinga" (To the Icelanders).[57] The Enlightenment luminary Magnús Stephensen had personified Iceland as an *eykona* as early as 1806.[58] But even this positive image can be tinged with sadness in patriotic poetry. The Island Woman in Thorsteinsson's poem is mournful because the heroic age has passed: 'Eykona hvít við dimmblátt djúp, / Er kappa vakir hrygg við hauga, / Þungbúnu hrýtur hagl af auga / Niður á fagran fannahjúp' (White Island Woman by the dark-blue deep, / Who holds a vigil over the mounds of heroes, / From her heavy eye a hard tear falls / Onto a beautiful shroud of snow).[59] Gone are the times, says the speaker who addresses the woman, 'þá konungborið

---

56 Joanna Szwajcowska, "The Myth of the Polish Mother", in *Women in Polish Cinema*, ed. Ewa Mazierska and Elzbieta Ostrowska (New York, Oxford: Berghahn Books, 2006), 15–33.
57 Thoroddsen, *Kvæði*, 13–21.
58 Magnús Stephensen, *Eptirmæli Atjándu Aldar eptir Krists híngadburd, frá Ey-konunni Islandi. I þessarar nafni framvørpud af Magnúsi Stephensen, Konúngl. Hátignar virkilegu Jústitsrádi og Justitiario í þeim konúngl. íslendska Lands-yfirretti* (Leirárgörðum við Leirá: Forlag Islands opinberu Vísinda-Stiptunar, 1806).
59 Thorsteinsson, *Ljóðmæli*, 98.

kappalið / kaus sér að deyja brjóst þitt við' (When a royal band of heroes / Chose to die on your bosom). The Mountain or Island Woman can be a motherly figure, as in Bjarni Thorarensen's "Íslands minni" ('Fair Mountain Woman! / You will be dear to your sons'), but she can also be like a symbol or an ideal without any real part to play: distant, and almost unattainable. The scholar Þorgerður H. Þorvaldsdóttir points out that the Mountain Woman and other images of women as symbolized in nationalistic discourse are not represented as active players but are passive in their reliance on men to save the day.[60] Steingrímur Thorsteinsson's poem "Ísland" is a good example of this attitude, as witnessed by the revealing address to the Island Woman: 'Kenn oss að feta í feðra spor / Á ferli nýjum, móðir aldna' (Teach us to follow in the fathers' footsteps / On a new course, old mother).[61] The woman is put on a pedestal as some kind of a goddess or mother figure to inspire men, but she is at the same time not in the position to be able to do anything herself. She simply serves as an ideal without any real power, and even if she wears a crown, and holds a sword, as in the image below, these are only symbols.

The elevated image of the Mountain Woman, symbolizing Iceland, corresponds to allegorical personifications like *Britannia* for Britain, *Germania* for Germany, *Marianne* for France, *Helvetia* for Switzerland, etc.[62] They became popular in the nineteenth century, not only in visual arts but also in literature. The scholar Þórir Óskarsson has pointed to the former national anthem of Switzerland, "Rufst du, mein Vaterland" (1811), by Johann Rudolf Wyss (1782–1830), as a parallel to Bjarni Thorarensen's "Íslands minni": 'Þar eins og í kvæði Bjarna er móðir þjóðarinnar, fjalladrottningin Helvetia, ákölluð, fegurð hennar lofsungin og minnt á náið og kærleiksríkt samband hennar við syni sína' (There, as in Bjarni's poem, the mother of the nation, the mountain queen Helvetia, is addressed, her beauty praised and one reminded of her intimate and loving relationship with her sons).[63] Whether the female personifications adopted by various nations were heroic, tragic, or beautiful embodiments of ideals, they were all

---

60 Þorgerður H. Þorvaldsdóttir, "Af fegurðardísum, ástandskonum og fjallkonum: Lesið í táknmyndir hins kvenlega í íslensku menningarumhverfi", in *Kvennaslóðir: Rit til heiðurs Sigríði Th. Erlendsdóttur sagnfræðingi*, Anna Agnarsdóttir, Erla Hulda Halldórsdóttir, Hallgerður Gísladóttir, Inga Huld Hákonardóttir, Sigríður Matthíasdóttir and Sigríður K. Þorgrímsdóttir, eds. (Reykjavík: Kvennasögusafn Íslands, 2001), 496.
61 Thorsteinsson, *Ljóðmæli*, 99.
62 Gunnell, "The Development and Role of the *Fjallkona* (Mountain Woman) in Icelandic National Day Celebrations and Other Contexts", 25; Smith, *Nationalism and Modernism*, 207–208.
63 Þórir Óskarsson, "Frá rómantík til raunsæis 1807–1882", in *Saga Íslands*, Vol. IX, Sigurður Líndal and Pétur Hrafn Árnason, eds. (Reykjavík: Hið íslenzka bókmenntafélag and Sögufélag, 2008), 395.

Ill. 2: Johann Baptist Zwecker (1814–1876), "Fjallkonan" (The Mountain Woman) – an engraving in the book *Icelandic Legends (Collected by Jón Arnason)* (London: Longmans, Green, & Co., 1866).

based on the same assumption of nationalism, namely that the people should acknowledge the homeland as a mother.

Conclusion: The Credo of Nationalism

Patriotic poems are written in accordance with the tenet or credo of nationalism, which holds that the nation and the land are closely bound. Those who read, perform, or sing such poems are supposed to identify with their homeland. This is what is meant by territorial kinship, or what Hans Kuhn calls a *pledge* in the context of Danish patriotic poetry.[64] As Guðrún Nordal points out in relation to Icelandic poems, kin and Earth become one in the very word *ættjörð*.[65] Many images and metaphors of territorial kinship in Icelandic patriotic poetry have already been discussed above, but a few may be added in order to show how Icelandic poets continued this tradition into the twentieth century.

These poets often tap into the metaphorical vein of the Icelandic language when describing the close connection with the land. Jóhannes úr Kötlum plays, for instance, upon the common usage of the word *berg* (rock), when someone's origins are being discussed. The way this is usually put in Icelandic is that someone is *(af tilteknu) bergi brotinn* (broken of a certain rock, i.e., stemming from somewhere).[66] Jóhannes turns this into a description of the Icelanders being a part of their land: 'ævi vor á jörðu hér / brot af þínu bergi er, / blik af þínum draumi' (Our life on this earth / Is a fragment of your rock, / A flash of your dream). The life of an Icelander is only a part of a larger continuum of land or nation, as the speaker in the poem not only pledges his allegiance to the land but also to the nation: 'hennar líf vér kjósum' (We choose its life). The metaphor combines life and land, but the discourse can also describe their connection as a mutual possession. In "Fylgd" (Escort) by Guðmundur Böðvarsson, a young son is addressed and reminded that he owns the land, just as the land owns him: 'En þú átt að muna, / alla tilveruna, / að þetta land á þig' (But you must remember, / All your life, / That this land owns you). This mutual possession of the land and the living is reminiscent of the description, in the "Prologue" to *The Prose Edda*, of the Earth as a mother.

The poet Stephan G. Stephansson, who emigrated to America as a young man, looked upon Iceland as his motherland/mother and Canada as his foster land/foster parent.[67] In his 1904 poem, "Úr Íslendingadags ræðu", he defined the Icelander's relationship with the old country in a revealing way:

> Þó þú langförull legðir
> sérhvert land undir fót,
> bera hugur og hjarta
> samt þíns heimalands mót,
> frænka eldfjalls og íshafs!
> sifji árfoss og hvers!

---

64 Kuhn, *Defining*, 126.
65 Nordal, "Landið", 108.
66 This particular usage seems to stem from stone cutting and originate in the Bible, according to Halldór Halldórsson, *Íslenzkt orðtakasafn*, Vol. I (Reykjavík: Almenna bókafélagið, 1968), 61, 343.
67 Guðrún Björk Guðsteinsdóttir, "'Ameríku-Stephán': 'reiðfantur á ótemju' tungunnar'", in *Skírnir* 170 (1996), 389–412, esp. 393–397.

dóttir langholts og lyngmós!
sonur landvers og skers!

(Though you travelled wide and far
And put your foot on every land,
Yet the mind and heart
Are moulded by your homeland,
Niece of volcano and polar sea!
Kin of river-fall and geyser!
Daughter of long-hill and heather-moor!
Son of oasis and skerry!)

This is like a family tree of territorial kinship (niece, kin, daughter, son), where the 'mind and heart' of each Icelander – however wide and far he or she travels – are moulded by the homeland and tied to the features of the landscape by a 'filial band'.[68]

To sum up, then, Icelandic patriotic poems are local versions of a type of poetry that became prominent because of eighteenth and nineteenth century European nationalism. They should be regarded as poetic genres belonging to a general patriotic discourse. Such poems are still popular, as they are frequently sung in various gatherings and convivial occasions in modern-day Iceland, despite lacking the historical or political significance they had during the time of the struggle for independence from Denmark, since Iceland became independent in 1918 and a republic in 1944. Perhaps it is ironic that the Icelanders should have learned the trade of patriotic poems from the nation they were writing and rebelling against. Danish writers had used a similar recipe since the early nineteenth century, when patriotic poems became somewhat standardized as discussed above. Later in the century, the Danish publisher of patriotic poems and national anthems Jacob Davidsen defined what they should include:

> En nationalsang må være en tolk for den kærlighed, der næres til fædrelandet, den må støtte og opildne denne kærlighed ved at fremhæve det lands fortrin og naturskønheder, hvor ens vugge stod, måske dvæle ved enkelte smukke historiske minder til opmuntring og efterligning, og overhoved i form og indhold være således digtet, at den kan tiltale enhver uden hensyn til stand eller alder, men fremfor alt, at den kan hævde sin vækkende og begejstrende kraft under alle tiders omskiftelser.[69]

---

68 The term 'filial band' is borrowed from Sir Walter Scott (1771–1832), who described the patriotic attachment to Scotland in a similar way in *The Lay of the Last Minstrel*, Canto Sixth (originally published in 1805): 'O Caledonia! stern and wild, / Meet nurse for a poetic child! / Land of brown heath and shaggy wood, / Land of the mountain and the flood, / Land of my sires! what mortal hand / Can e'er untie the filial band, / That knits me to thy rugged strand!' *The Lay of the Last Minstrel, A Poem; By Walter Scott, Esq.* (London: Longman, Hurst, Rees, and Orme, 1810), 176.

69 Jacob Davidsen, "En kronet Nationalsang", in *Fra vore Fædres Tid: Skildringer og Skitser* (Copenhagen: Gyldendal, 1884), 94.

(A national anthem must be an interpreter for the love that is nurtured for the fatherland; it must support and incite this love by highlighting the merits and natural beauties of that country, where one's cradle stood, perhaps dwell on some beautiful historical memories for encouragement and imitation, and generally in form and content be written in such a way as to appeal to anyone regardless of position or age, but first and foremost, that it may assert its rousing and exhilarating power despite the vicissitudes of historical change.)

This is roughly the recipe used in Icelandic patriotic poems as well. The emphasis is on a general – not a particular – description, and on celebrating one's love for the homeland. A nation is an imagined community, as Benedict Anderson has famously stated. Nowhere does this become clearer than in poetry written with the purpose of rallying people around the concept of the nation. The common denominator in this is the land, which is described in general terms, so it can appeal to 'anyone regardless of position or age', as Davidsen says. This is the way in which patriotic poems give the imagined community a voice and a ground – expression and basis – and encourage people to celebrate their nationality. They all have the same roots and are related, because they have a common mother or father, which is the homeland. This is the persistent myth of nationalism, and as long as patriotic poems are read, performed, or sung, it will continue to work its way into the hearts and minds of people around the world.

Helena Bergmann
(University of Borås)

Cross-Channel Motions: The Educational Writings of Mary Hays Versus Those of Pauline de Meulan-Guizot

Abstract

The current paper seeks to investigate the achievements of two female writers from two European countries of the late eighteenth and early nineteenth centuries. Mary Hays and Pauline de Meulan-Guizot were both highly involved in the issue of education, albeit from separate angles. The British author, Mary Hays, an adept of Godwinian and Helvetian philosophies, emphasized the need for schooling in general and for girls in particular. Most of her writings were dedicated to the cause of female liberation. In France, Pauline de Meulan-Guizot wrote several pedagogical and didactic works, both together with her husband, the liberal politician François Guizot, and independently. Her writings were mainly focused on the moral upbringing of the young. The aim of this study is to compare the different outlooks of the two writers as well as to identify the links between them.

Keywords

Hays, de Meulan-Guizot, education, female emancipation, conduct literature

Introduction

Conduct books for children, with the 'raison d'être' of providing 'the most efficient means for shaping individuals', had started appearing already in the sixteenth century.[1] By the second half of the eighteenth century the interest in writing for didactic purposes had turned into a major European trend. The most influential manifestation of its kind was Jean-Jacques Rousseau's pedagogical tract, *Émile, ou de l'Éducation* (*Emile, or On Education*) from 1762, voicing the conviction that the best way for a child to gain an education was by living in close contact with nature.[2] While Rousseau focussed on the constructive and edifying upbringing of young boys, his recommendations for young girls were of a more restrictive kind. In the final years of the 18th century, however, there was an

---

1 Nancy Armstrong, *Desire and Domestic Fiction: A Political History of the Novel* (Oxford: Oxford University Press, 1987), 100.
2 Rousseau, Jean-Jacques, *Èmile ou de l'Èducation* (A La Hay: Chez Jean Néaulme, 1762).

increased interest in didactic books intended specifically for young girls. Although female authors were the anticipated proponents of this genre, it was Doctor John Gregory's *A Father's Legacy to his Daughters*, published in 1774, that gave the conduct book a real breakthrough in England.[3] A vital constituent of his advice to parents was that their daughters should abstain from trying to match, or supersede, the intellectual powers of young men. His convictions won approval among the majority of his readership, but were strongly refuted by the author-to-be of *A Vindication of the Rights of Woman* (1792), Mary Wollstonecraft (1759-1797).[4] Dr Gregory's conservative views prompted her to publish her own handbook on parenting: *Thoughts on the Education of Daughters* (1787), which became the starting-point of her career as a feminist icon.

Mary Wollstonecraft's involvement in the issue of female emancipation was deeply shared by her friend, the radical writer Mary Hays (1759-1843), author of *Appeal to the Men of Great Britain in Behalf of Women* (1798). Less adversarial than Wollstonecraft's, Hays's work was more socio-politically focussed on creating a better understanding between the sexes. Elements of 'didacticism' were tangible components of her works of fiction, too. In her novel *Memoirs of Emma Courtney* (1796), she expresses particular concern for the necessity of keeping a balance between 'reason' and 'feeling', so as to avoid succumbing to female submissiveness during interactions with the opposite sex .[5]

Since the background of *Memoirs of Emma Courtney* was partly autobiographical in its exposure of an unrequited love affair, Mary Hays's novel was viewed by many with a degree of ostracism.[6] However, as English literary works were becoming increasingly popular in France, her novel was among those selected for translation into French. The translator was Elizabeth Charlotte Pauline de Meulan (1773-1827), a young Parisian of aristocratic lineage, who had taken on the task of making foreign literary works available in her own language to support her family after the Revolution.[7] There were no laws to protect foreign authors at the time, so what appeared in France had often been vastly altered.[8]

---

3 Dr. John Gregory, *A Father's Legacy to his Daughters* (London: W. Straman & T.Cadell, 1774).
4 Wollstonecraft's feminist didacticism was manifested also in her two literary works: *Mary a Fiction* (1788), promoting female ingenuity, and the unfinished *Maria: or, The Wrongs of Woman* (1790/98), exposing the ills of domestic brutality.
5 The significance of this dualism was substantiated through Mary Hays overt referencing to the Unitarian philosophy of William Godwin (1756-1836) and to the utilitarianism of Claude-Adrien Helvetius (1715-1751) in her novel.
6 The man Mary Hays had an emotional attachment with was the respected Unitarian tutor and Cambridge lecturer William Frend (1757-1841).
7 Pauline de Meulan's translation was named: *La Chapelle d'Ayton, ou Emma Courtney* and published in 1799.
8 *The French Literary and Artistic Property Act of 1793* did not apply to works from abroad.

Although Mary Hays and Pauline de Meulan (later known as Pauline Guizot) came from separate cultures and had different outlooks on both literary form and content, they did have a common cause to unite them: their deep involvement in the welfare of the young.[9] This was an era when 'women were increasingly constructed as the ideal educators of children' and concern for the moral upbringing of the young was an area they both shared.[10] At the same time, they were united through their readiness to be 'socially transgressive' in daring to move outside the realm of fiction by entering also the strictly 'male' sphere of journalistic writing.[11]

Unitarian Didactics in London

Mary Hays's works for the young generation were deeply preoccupied with moral issues. The first of her primarily 'didactic' writings, was an abbreviated version of Henry Brooke's sentimental picaresque novel from 1777, *The Fool of Quality or the History of Henry Earl of Mooreland*, which she granted the eponymous title of *Harry Clinton; or, a Tale of Youth* (1804).[12] The didactic theme of this story is that the poor should be treated with dignity, a message of special social concern to Hays. Therefore, the challenge she offers her main character, Harry Clinton, is of a moral nature requiring him to choose the right decisions when, under the surveillance of his wealthy benefactor, he has been given the task of distributing money to the poor.

Mary Hays was a devoted member of the Unitarian Church, the main theoretical cornerstone of which was the rejection of the Christian doctrine of the Trinity. This meant viewing God as an entity and not as a division between the Father, the Son, and the Holy Spirit. The Unitarians saw Christ as a saviour, but denied his Divinity.[13] What characterised the Church particularly was their egalitarian view on education. Ruth Watts, in *Gender, Power and the Unitarians*, affirms 'that Unitarianism played a significant role in changing the ideas on

---

9 Pauline de Meulan married the liberal, protestant politician François Guizot (1787–1874) in 1812.
10 Rebecka Davies, *Written Maternal Authority and Eighteenth-Century Education in Britain: Educating by the Book* (Farnham, Surrey and Burlington, VT: Ashgate, 2014), 5.
11 Carla Hesse, *The Other Enlightenment: How French Women Became Modern* (Princeton and Oxford: Princeton University Press, 2003), 47.
12 Text supplied by Whelan, Timothy, "Mary Hays, Life, Writings and Correspondence" (2018). www.maryhayslifewritingcorrespondence.com/.
13 The first English Unitarian congregation was founded in London by Theodophilus Linsdey in 1774. See Tuggy, Dale, "Trinity" in *The Stanford Encyclopedia of Philosophy*, ed. Edward N. Zalta (Winter 2021 Edition). https://plato.stanford.edu/archives/win2021/entries/trinity/.

women's abilities and what they could do.'[14] Hence, it was in this congregation that Mary Hays found support for her vision of making education available to everyone regardless of gender.

Most of Mary Hays's didactic stories were written for adolescents and not for the very young. Her three-volume work *Historical Dialogues for Young Persons* (1806–07) was advertised as

> not intended for children ... but for youth, from the age of twelve years and upwards; and also, as a recreation, or exercise, for the elder pupils in schools, where the author has been encouraged to hope, by several of their respectable conductors, that it may prove an acceptable present.[15]

A characteristic scenario of the didactic genre was the use of blatant character opposites, such as in her moral dramatization: *The Brothers; or, Consequences: A Story of what Happens Every Day; Addressed to that most useful Part of the Community, the Labouring Poor* (1815).[16] Written as a play, it begins in a comical fashion, with a mother trying to guide her two sons of entirely different inclinations towards achieving a stable and responsible life. William follows his mother's advice and finds a like-minded and sensible spouse, while the choices made by the frivolous Robert draw him only into tragedy and dissipation. The underlying moral message of the story emerges in a quote from Ecclesiasticus XXXV, v. 9 on the title page: 'If thou hast gathered nothing in thy youth, how can'st thou find anything in thine age?' To her later editions of this story, Hays adjoined some more concrete information on the topic of investing money in Savings Banks, an illustration of a personal form of pecuniary didactics, aimed specifically at helping the less prosperous members of the community.

Mary Hays's *Family Annals or The Sisters*, published in 1817, offers warnings against the pitfalls of adolescence. This time her story centres on girls with dichotomous personalities: Ellen and Charlotte, one generous and caring, the other irresponsible and daring. Ellen settles into marriage with a loyal partner, in bucolic harmony, which is accentuated through repeated insertions of lines from Mary Hays's favourite poet during her youth: James Thompson's "The Seasons." Conversely, Charlotte, governed entirely by 'Passions', declares that 'love and cottage would in less than six months kill her with ennui,' an attitude which dooms her to a dark and desperate end.[17]

---

14 Ruth Watts *Gender, Power and the Unitarians in England 1760–1860* (London: Longman, 1998),1.
15 Mary Hays, *Historical Dialogues for Young Persons* (London: J. Johnson, 1806).
16 Text supplied by Whelan, Timothy, 2018. *Mary Hays, Life, Writings and Correspondence.* Retrieved February 28, 2019, from *www.maryhayslifewritingcorrespondence.com/*.
17 Mary Hays, "Family Annals, or the Sisters" in *Mary Hays, Life, Writings and Correspondence*, ed. Whelan, Timothy (London: W. Simpkin and R. Marshall, 1817). www.maryhayslifewritingcorrespondence.com/.

Outside the specific genre of dogmatic conduct books, most of Mary Hays's writings were, essentially, 'didactic'. Both *Memoirs of Emma Courtney* and her second novel, *The Victim of Prejudice*, were written in support of female liberation. The ending of *Emma Courtney* offers a message of hope for the generations to come, prefiguring a future in which 'men begin to think and reason' preparing themselves to enjoy the advantages of a life on equal terms. There will be a time, Hays assures her readers, when 'reformation dawns, though the advance is tardy'.[18] A similar pedagogical avowal is made in *The Victim of Prejudice*, which ends with its main character, Mary Raymond, asserting that she would '*have lived in vain!* unless the stories of [her] sorrows should kindle in the heart of man, in behalf of [her] suppressed sex, the sacred claims of humanity and justice'.[19] Gina Luria Walker, underscoring the wider significance of this particular novel suggests that it emphasises 'a common bond among women, based on gender that reaches beyond friendship between individual women into a community, to the possibility of collective female cooperation'.[20]

Mary Hays's journalistic achievements proved yet another channel for her emancipatory urgings. In 'Improvements suggested in Female Education', published in *The Monthly Magazine and British Register for 1797*, she reinforces that girls must

> be devoted to the attainment of some ingenious art and useful trade by which a young woman might hope to gain an honest and honourable independence and be freed from the disgraceful necessity of bartering her person to procure a maintenance.[21]

Her most articulate and pragmatic call for female emancipation was her tract *Appeal to the Men of Great Britain in Behalf of Women*, originally formulated in 1790, and published in 1798. Unlike her close friend Mary Wollstonecraft's *A Vindication of the Rights of Woman*, Hays's tract underscores the value of compromise, as a prerequisite for the accomplishment of sound companionship between the sexes. Her message, 'educational' rather than reproachful, was intended to highlight the benefits to be had for both parties if ready to live on equal terms.

In the central chapter of *Appeal to the Men of Great Britain* named "Of the Erroneous Ideas that Men have formed, of the Characters and Abilities of Women", Hays sharpens her didactics by applying a pedagogy of stimulant and reward to encourage egalitarianism within the household: 'I most firmly believe

---

18 Mary Hays, *Memoirs of Emma Courtney* (London: G.G. and J. Robinson, 1796), 189.
19 Mary Hays, *The Victim of Prejudice* (London: J. Johnson, 1799), 174.
20 Gina Luria Walker, *Mary Hays (1759–1843) The Growth of a Woman's Mind* (London: Ashgate, 2006), 194.
21 Mary Hays, "Improvements suggested in Female Education" in *The Monthly Magazine and British Register for 1797*, 194.

that *good humor* is *one* of the happy consequences, to be reasonably expected if women were everywhere put on a rational and equitable footing'.[22] Her *Memoirs of Emma Courtney* offered a similarly optimistic vision of a future allowing men and women to 'emancipate the human mind from the trammels of superstition', meaning from archaic perceptions of gender. Instead she promotes the idea of working together 'with mingled branches', that is, on equal terms.[23]

Aristocratic Pedagogy in Paris

Three years after its publication, *Memoirs of Emma Courtney* was translated into French by Pauline de Meulan.[24] Her adaptation of Mary Hays's novel was extremely well received by the French readership and enabled her to support her mother and siblings through the use of her pen. By 1801 she had established herself as a respected critic, writing for the Paris journal, *Le Publiciste,* on the subjects of the theatre, literature, society and morals.[25] In the same year, she published a collection of stories intended for children: *Les Enfans: Contes à l'Usage de la Jeunesse* (children: stories intended for the young), now under her married name of Guizot.

Both Mary Hays and Pauline Guizot acknowledged the efficacy of specially adapted forms of literature to help shape the young into harmonious law-abiding citizens. Pauline's strong concern for the future was shared by her husband, François Guizot, a respected philosopher and holder of many important functions in French society.[26] Mary Hays, although frequently discussing with both Mary Wollstonecraft and William Godwin, had forwarded her pedagogical ideas independently. Conversely, the Guizots, known for their 'lasting intellectual fellowship', authored stories and articles for the journal *Le Publiciste* together. This was followed by their pedagogical venture *Annales de l'Éducation* (annals of education) (1811–1814), a monthly periodical containing fictitious diary entries on the theme of a mother's concern for her daughters, and promoting the idea of 'a mother educator' in the home.[27]

---

22 Mary Hays, *Appeal to the Men of Great Britain in Behalf of Women* (London: J. Johnson, 1798), 293.
23 Mary Hays, *Memoirs of Emma Courtney* (London: G. G. and J. Robinson, 1796), 199.
24 Pauline de Meulan, *La Chapelle d'Ayton ou Emma Courtney* (Paris: Maradan, 1799).
25 The journal *Le Publiciste* was issued between 1797–1810. See Nadine Bérenguier, *Conduct Books for Girls in Enlightenment France* (London: Ashgate, 2011) 198, for de Meulans contributions.
26 François Guizot (1787–1784). A liberal politician and professor of history at the University of Sorbonne, later also Minister of Education.
27 Karen Offen, *The Woman Question in France 1400–1870* (Cambridge: Cambridge University Press, 2017), 131.

Most of Pauline Guizot's didactic writings were written in response to the horrors experienced by the bourgeoisie during the Revolution. Devoting herself to 'moral activities,' she made it her mission to work proactively to help prevent any renewed outbreak of political violence in France. Her aim was to influence inhabitants at an early and malleable stage of their lives, and she was convinced that writing fictional stories with a moral message for specific age-groups would serve this end. Also, she strove to promote an educational system governed by reason, which should be effectuated, not through reprimands, but, inspired by Rousseau, through competent guidance that would engender an ability to make sensible decisions.

In 1821, Pauline Guizot published her most famous work, *L'Écolier ou Raoul et Victor,* a novel for adolescents intended to stall tendencies of violence and self-will. The book was awarded a prize as *the best book of the year* by L'Académie Française. When, twenty years later, it was translated into English as *The Young Student, or Ralph and Victor,* it was was greeted by critics as 'a perfect reflecting mirror ... precisely fitted to meliorate ... youth ... and direct their course', towards 'subordination to the higher authority of Christian ethics'.[28] *L'Écolier ou Raoul et Victor* begins with a chapter entitled "The Storm", an implied reference to social turmoil and violence. The reader is introduced to the restless Raoul, to whom 'all rules were intolerable'.[29] He is intelligent yet characterised by a 'folly and obstinacy' that 'neither scholastic discipline, nor the lessons taught him by his comrades, nor the dread of his father, had been able to subdue'.[30] In defiance, Raoul drops out of school, leaves home and joins up with Victor, another renegade 'of respectable family, who had received a good education, but, who, led away by his bad disposition', had committed a felony by 'entering a lady's house and stealing a diamond ring'.[31] A clear reference from the author to the pillaging that was carried out against the aristocracy during the Revolution.

The two wayward young gentlemen face many an adventure as they join up and collaborate with bandits and smugglers. Finally, shamed by their wrong-doings, they return home, after Victor has restored the stolen ring to its rightful owner. The lesson learned is that freedom that causes pain to others can never be justified or fulfilling. This anti-revolutionary message is delivered in convoluted form through Raoul's epiphany on his journey home: 'his youth bore him onward; his youth still unabated; seemed to him unbounded, and yet he did not feel free. Liberty only exists to him to whom it legitimately belongs'.[32] This choice of allegory mirrors the author's own fear of Jacobinism.

---

28 Translated by Samuel Jackson in 1845 and reviewed in the *New York Courier & Enquirer.*
29 Pauline Guizot, *L'Écolier ou Raoul et Victor* (Paris: Chez Ladvocat Librairie, 1821), 5.
30 Guizot, *L'Écolier,* 2.
31 Guizot, *L'Écolier,* 36.
32 Guizot, *L'Écolier,* 69.

Pedagogical Divergences

After the success of her prize-winning novel, Pauline Guizot authored several collections of stories for the young, such as *Nouveaux Contes* (new tales) and *Nouvelles et Contes pour la Jeunesse* (short stories and tales for the young).[33] Her didactic work intended for parents, instigated as a dialogue between an aunt and her niece, *L'Éducation Domestique ou Lettres de Famille* (education at home or family letters), awarded her a second prize by *L'Académie Française*.[34] Her work professed that, in the upbringing of the very young, there should be no gender differences. Yet, for children over five, recommendations were different. According to Pauline Guizot, girls need not gain the same education as boys, but should acquire an 'ability to think independently, which rote study would never facilitate'.[35] Ideally, they should be taught at home until the age of twelve, learning dressmaking and how to care for household economy. Her views were a far cry from those voiced in Mary Hays's *Appeal to the Men of Great Britain:*

> Many a good head is stuffed with ribbons, gauze, fringes, flounces and furbelows, that might have received or communicated, far other and noble impressions. And many a fine imagination has been exhausted upon these, which had they been turned to the study of nature or initiated into the dignified embellishments of the fine arts, might have adorned, delighted, and improved society.[36]

For Hays, attaining equality in education between boys and girls was an overall mission. For Guizot, it was the societal content that mattered, since politically holding the country together was of tantamount importance. Regardless, both educationalists shared disbelief in the power of castigation as a pedagogical method of improvement. In *Letters and Essays, Moral and Miscellaneous*, Hays professes that she 'trembles' at the thought of 'the future moral conduct of the child whom force and blows only could refrain from doing what was wrong'.[37]

Mary Hays had an extraordinary trust in the times to come. Even on hearing of the Revolution, her reaction was reluctantly hopeful, as she writes in her *Letters and Essays, Moral and Miscellaneous:* 'Posterity will, I have no doubt, reap the benefits of the present struggles in France, but they are ruinous and dreadful to

---

33 See Pauline Guizot, *Nouveaux Contes* (Paris: Didier, 1823) Pauline Guizot, *Nouvelles et Contes pour la Jeunesse* (Limoges: Eugène Ardent et Cie, 1827).
34 See Pauline Guizot, *L'Education Domestique ou Lettres de Famille sur l'Education* (Paris: Leroux et Constant-Chantpie, 1826).
35 Rogers, Rebecka, *From the Salon to the Schoolroom: Educating Bourgeois Girls in Nineteenth Century France* (The Pennsylvania atate University Press: University Park Pennsylvania, 2005) 29.
36 Hays, Mary, *An Appeal to the Men of Great Britain in Behalf of Women* (London: J. Johnson, 1798) 79.
37 Hays, *Letters and Essays Moral and Miscellaneous* (London: J. Johnson, 1793) 97.

those actually engaged in them'.[38] Similarly, the construction of a tragic end to her novel *Memoirs of Emma Courtney* carries with it a disguised hope for the future. Here, Hays lets Emma the younger, the daughter of her main character, die prematurely, as though symbolically, in abeyance of a society ready to offer young women a better life. Conversely, Pauline de Meulan's *La Chapelle d'Ayton ou Emma Courtney*, whose main aim was to restore traditional values and provide delectable reading, allows her French Emma to dance her way through ballrooms, picking and choosing among admirers, until finally safely ensconced in a happy marriage.

Although pertaining to the same heroine, these two works were very different from one another. The one initially a compensatory attempt to fictionalise an authentic, unrequited love affair, the other a manifest denial that a woman should ever need to undergo the deception of being jilted. Two authors joined to one another through their literary undertakings, one of which as a consequence as well as an antithesis of the other. Mary Hays and Pauline Guizot may have had diverse outlooks on the realities of female existence, but there was vital major cause that unified them: their strong concern for the future of the young in their respective societies. If in the 21st century, Mary Hays's appeals have faded into the past, this is thanks to the latter-day achievements of the emancipatory movements she herself had helped to initiate. Pauline Guizot's works, however, have remained part of the French literary-pedagogical canon for the young. Ever appearing in new editions that are still being read and enjoyed at schools to this day.

---

38 Ibid., 17.

Anne Jerslev
(University of Copenhagen)

David Lynch and the Fragment[1]

Abstract
The article engages with American artist and filmmaker David Lynch's audio-visual fragments. I argue that it makes sense to go back to the theory of the early romantic writers, and in particular Friedrich Schlegel, to think through the fragments in Lynch's works. Starting from a short discussion of Lynch's use of the word fragment, the article proceeds to outline Schlegel's seminal, late 18th century writing about the fragment as well as some of the recent discussions of the concept. The final part of the article goes into fragments from some of Lynch's films as well as from his 2017 TV series *Twin Peaks: The Return* in order to argue that using the fragment as an analytical tool removes the focus from looking for – impossible – coherence in Lynch's works and instead focuses on how the fragmented structure contributes to creating the aesthetic surplus and affective atmosphere with which the director's *oeuvre* is so rich.

Keywords
fragment, romanticism, atmosphere, affect, aesthetic

Introduction

When describing his creative process, American film director and multimedia-artist David Lynch often uses the terms 'fragments' and 'ideas' interchangeably. An idea always comes as a fragment. Fragments feed other fragments, which may eventually compile into something. However, the structure is not decided from the beginning:

> You see, I get ideas in fragments, and only when a bunch of fragments come together I say: "Oh, this is about this, or this could be about this." But there's absolutely no

---
1 This article is an abbreviated and slightly rewritten version of Chapter 6 in my book *David Lynch: Blurred Boundaries* (Palgrave Macmillan, 2021), which is an inter-media discussion of Lynch's work. Permission to print is kindly granted by Palgrave Macmillan.

message, no steering anyone any which way. I just love the idea. I want to realise them [ideas] because I'm in love with them.[2]

The fragment can be seen as an aesthetic figure of interruption in Lynch's narratives. Yet, interruption might not be the right word for a recurrent form in his works. Fragments are spaces of aesthetic and affective force in a context in which narrative development can be regarded as secondary, a necessity for transporting the viewer from one fragment to another. In this article I use the fragment to think through the ways Lynch's works speaks to contemporary anxieties. How he constructs spaces characterized by destabilization and discontinuity, perceptual disorientation, and uncertainty. How he defamiliarizes the familiar and how he opposes textual coherence in the classical cinema sense of unity and causality to instead create a processual and performative textuality. Accordingly, I ask how the deployment of scholarly conceptualizations of the fragment can contribute to the analysis of a Lynch work which aims at highlighting the condensed atmospheres of single parts instead of looking for coherence and a meaningful whole.

I address this question by, first, sketching Lynch's description of his creative process, and I discuss what he himself means by 'idea' and 'fragment'. In the ensuing theoretical section, I outline the early romantic ideas of the fragment in Schlegel's late eighteenth-century writing, and I include more recent discussion of the fragment as a kind of writing in between culture's fields of enunciation.[3] In the third part of the article, I analyse two fragments from *Wild at Heart* (1990) and two from *Twin Peaks: The Return* (2017) which share with many other Lynch fragments an atmosphere of intensity resulting from the destabilization of space.[4] My concluding point is not to argue that David Lynch is a belated romanticist, though. Rather, thinking through the Romantic fragment as a textually ambiguous form and how it echoes in Lynch's work makes it possible to conclude on how the powerful disorder and affective spaces in Lynch's works transgress and challenge established cultural and aesthetic dichotomies.

Thinking of Lynch's audio-visual works as being held together by fragments makes it possible to think of entering a *network* in which any possible totality is lost from view and from which there is no obvious entry point and exit. The illuminated exit sign that we find a few times in Lynch (most significantly in the club in which Fred Madison plays his sax in *Lost Highway* (1997)) may be re-

---

2 Killian Fox, "Interview: David Lynch: It's important to go out and feel the so-called reality" in *The Guardian* (London, United Kingdom), 30 June. https://www.theguardian.com/film/2019/jun/30/david-lynch-interview-manchester-international-festival.
3 Horace Engdahl, "Anteckningar om fragmentet" in *Stilen och lyckan*, ed. Horace Engdahl (Stockholm: Bonniers, 1992 [1988]), 27–44.
4 Anne Jerslev, *David Lynch: Blurred Boundaries* (Cham, Schwitzerland: Palgrave Macmillan, 2021).

garded as an ironic comment on what is not present in Lynch's spaces. Thus, the proper analytical approach to Lynch's work is not thinking of unravelling a complex puzzle. The pieces of Lynch's work are not meant to take their one and only place in the completion of a predetermined pattern. The fragment is not just a piece of a puzzle but a whole in itself, however blurred its boundaries may be to its textual surrounding. I suggest calling these fragments of compressed intensity or pieces of 'concentrated text'[5] for *affective spaces*, drawing on German philosopher Gernot Böhme's thinking of spaces and atmospheres as understood 'in terms of the affects they arouse in specific situations'[6] and Böhme inspired cultural-geographer Ben Anderson[7] who talks about atmospheres as spaces 'of intensity that overflows a represented world organized into subjects and objects or subjects and other subjects'.[8] As Anderson wrote, 'atmospheres are singular affective qualities that emanate from but exceed the assembling of bodies'.[9] In David Lynch's fragments audio-visual atmospheres are created by aesthetic means.

'I Always Go by Ideas'

To Lynch, an idea is not a theme or a segment of a narrative. Ideas are moods attached to an abstraction, a simple contour of something to which can be added something else, just like Lynch said about catching the idea for *Lost Highway* (1997): '[T]hen I told Barry [author Barry Gifford] an idea that had come to me the last night of shooting *Fire Walk with Me*. And it was *the videotapes* and *a couple*. And Barry loved this idea'.[10] Thus, ideas are not fragments of narrative: 'videotapes and a couple' designate rather a percept, a simple tableau, or a blurred still photo waiting to gain sharpness and come alive.

In Lynch, an idea is at once a part of a whole and comprises the whole: 'An idea comes. You get an idea and the idea tells you everything'.[11] Ideas are unique

---

5 Maurice Blanchot, "The Athenaeum" *Studies in Romanticism 22, no. 2* (Summer 1983), 172. https://doi.org/10.2307/25600425.
6 Gernot Böhme, *The Aesthetics of Atmospheres* (London & New York: Routledge, 2017), 183.
7 Ben Anderson, "Affective Atmospheres", *Emotion, Space and Society 2* (December 2009), 77–81. https://doi.org/10.1016/j.emospa.2009.08.005; Ben Anderson, *Encountering Affect* (New York and London: Routledge, 2016).
8 Anderson, "Affective Atmospheres", 79; Anderson, *Encountering Affect*, 174.
9 Anderson, "Affective Atmospheres", 80.
10 Chris Douridas, "Interview" in *David Lynch interviews,* ed. Richard A. Barney (Jackson: University Press of Mississippi, 2009 [2006]), 150. My italics.
11 John Esther, "David Lynch and Laura Dern: *Inland Empire*" in *David Lynch interviews* ed. Richard E. Barney (Jackson: University Press of Mississippi, 2009 [2006]), 247.

'sparks'[12] that float around and can be caught like catching a fish in Lynch's own repetitive metaphoric language.[13] His creative mantras seem to be intuition, an open mind to whatever idea comes around and being 'true' to that idea.

Lynch has often been asked whether it is true that his latest movie *Inland Empire* (2006) departed from a long monologue performed by actress Laura Dern that he shot as a completed scene. In one interview he answers that 'in the beginning there was no *Inland Empire*, no idea of a feature. All there was was an idea for a scene, that's it'.[14] In another interview about the film Lynch elaborates on what happens once an idea has entered his creative mind:

> So I'm looking at it and I say, "No, this isn't just a scene, this holds something more". And I think about it. In the meantime, though, I got another idea, and I wrote it down, and shot that. And that was actually two different scenes. And those scenes did not relate to the scene we were talking about .... Then, I got another idea, and I wrote it out, and shot that scene, and it didn't relate at all to what had gone before, not a bit. It did in a way, because it was the same character, but it didn't really. But there was something – I was still thinking about the previous scenes, but they did not relate, *at all*.[15]

Accordingly, puzzle and pieces of the puzzle are not proper metaphors for either Lynch's creative process or his works. Depending upon the number of ideas he 'falls in love' with, as he keeps saying, the pieces – or fragments – can be put in many places in the network, which constitutes a contingent whole at any one time. They may be removed and stored and then reappear in some other work or as an independent fragment. Apparently, anything can happen until the very end.

The many fragments of which *Twin Peaks: The Return* consists never add up to a coherent whole. *Twin Peaks: The Return* in essence provides the impression of a work that is in a process of becoming or change, of fragments that may combine with other fragments into an entirety held together by the one-hour episode format. Even though Lynch himself operates with a sense of closure ('it's not finished until it's finished' he has said on several occasions),[16] his departure from 'ideas' that come to him, pushes everything else aside and then multiplies and combines in different ways, makes it difficult to close a project: 'Who's to say

---

12 Laurent Tirard, *Moviemakers' Master Class: Private Lessons from the World's Foremost Directors* (New York: Farrar, Straus and Giroux, 2002).
13 David Lynch, *Catching the Big Fish. Meditation, Consciousness, and Creativity* (New York: Jeremy P. Tarcher/Penguin, 2006).
14 Richard E. Barney, "*Inland Empire*, Transcendental Meditation, and the "Swim" of Ideas" in *David Lynch Interviews,* ed. Richard E. Barney (Jackson: University Press of Mississippi, 2009), 253.
15 Barney, "Inland Empire", 254; for a similar quote see Esther, "David Lynch", 247.
16 Gaby Wood and Hazel Sheffield, "The Interview: David Lynch" in *The Guardian* (London, United Kingdom), 1 March. https://www.theguardian.com/film/2009/feb/28/david-lynch-twin-peaks-mulholland-drive.

whether the waiting for the final piece could open up another whole thing that was meant to be?'.[17] In Lynch's way of working, a whole might not be a whole at all.

Swedish literary scholar Horace Engdahl suggests provocatively following Derrida that any text may be considered a fragment.[18] Accordingly, Engdahl continues, one could argue that there is no such thing as a fragment, and neither is there such thing as a textual whole. Along the same line, Germanist Justus Fetscher, echoing Schlegel, claims that 'every text is in essence fragment, every fragment text'.[19] Though Engdahl does not subscribe to the radicality in this claim, he argues that even the shortest text consists of a diversity of texts that are each related to one another. Evidently, David Lynch's films each constitute a whole. They have a title; they are distributed as stand-alone works and are treated by the institution of critics as such. However, what give the films and the TV series their form are their different ways of constituting an aesthetics of fragmentation. Fragments are evidently – for the above reason – assembled to constitute a whole but arguing for coherence in an audio-visual Lynch work is, in my opinion, not as interesting as exploring the audio-visual richness in the fragments. I consider the entire Lynch work as being composed of fragments of different sizes and forms, which unite to different degrees. However, I also see it in a paradoxical way as a fragmentary totality.[20]

Lynch describes the fragment as a contradictory aesthetic form, which is, on the one hand, a self-sufficient entity with a force of its own but on the other hand also partakes of a larger aesthetic context: 'When you only see a part, it's even stronger than seeing the whole. The whole might have a logic, but out of its context, the fragment takes on a tremendous value of abstraction'.[21] The de-contextualized, self-sufficient fragment is aesthetically and emotionally powerful. Undoubtedly, in Lynch's many remarks about ideas and fragments, distinctions between the part and the whole are blurred. On the one hand, the fragment is never self-enclosed. It always partakes of a larger whole to which it is connected more or less loosely. On the other hand, the whole is never a coherent bounded whole. As such, fragments are tied to the overall narrative but also punctuate it.

---

17 Lynch in Justus Nieland, *David Lynch* (Urbana, Chicago & Springfield: University of Illinois Press, 2012), 168.
18 Engdahl, "Anteckningar".
19 Justus Fetscher, "Tendency, Disintegration, Decay: Stages of the Aesthetics of the Fragment from Friedrich Schlegel to Thomas Bernhard" in *The Aesthetics of the Total Artwork: on Borders and Fragments,* ed. Anke Finger and Danielle Follet (Baltimore: The Johns Hopkins University Press, 2011), 53.
20 See Jerslev, *Blurred Boundaries* for extended discussions of the Lynch oeuvre, including his paintings, photography, music videos, YouTube material, etc.
21 Chris Rodley, *Lynch on Lynch. Revised edition* (New York: Farrar, Straus and Giroux, 2005 [1997]), 231.

Fragments function by themselves and have an aesthetic and affective power of their own.

The Fragment in Romantic and Contemporary Theory

Across more than two centuries, reading some of early Romantic writer Friedrich Schlegel's fragments is like listening to Lynch talking: 'Every system *grows* out of fragments'.[22] Likewise, Schlegel writes in fragment 808: 'All poetic fragments must in some way be parts of a whole'.[23] In the same way, reading Lynch's statements in interviews is like reading Schlegel aphorisms: 'When you only see a part, it's even stronger than seeing the whole.' The following sentence in the same quote sounds as another aphorism: 'The whole might have a logic, but out of its context, the fragment takes on a tremendous value of abstraction.' Again: I am not arguing that Lynch is after all an early romantic. However, I am arguing that the so-called Jena romantics' famous fragments written and published around the year 1800 offer a useful basis for thinking through Lynch's way of hardly telling a story or at least not telling a straight out coherent story in his audiovisual works.[24]

Both above sentences concern the part and the whole or the singular and the totality. Hereby, they connect with Schlegel's aphorisms or what he himself called fragments, which were published over a short period between 1797 and 1800 in *Lyceum Fragments* or *Critical Fragments* (1797), *Athenaeum Fragments* (1798) and *Ideas* (1800). Schlegel writes illuminatingly, for example, in one of his *Critical* fragments (no. 14): 'In poetry too every whole can be a part and every part really a whole'.[25] This way of thinking about the part and the whole as complementary instead of mutually exclusive forms, even thinking that there is no whole that is not also a part, also informs the Lynch quotes. Schlegel is occupied with thinking through a system that tones down system and coherence without excluding system and coherence altogether. Moreover, like Schlegel's writing, Lynch's fragmented speech in interviews often takes the form of aphorisms, at

---

22 From fragment 496. See Friedrich von Schlegel and Hans Eichner, *Kritische Friedrich Schlegel Ausgabe* XVI (Paderborn, München, Wien: Ferdinand Schöning Verlag, 1981), 126. Italics in original.
23 Schlegel and Eichner, *Kritische Friedrich Schlegel Ausgabe XVI,* 154.
24 In Eric G. Wilson, "Sickness unto Death: David Lynch & Sacred Irony" in *David Lynch in Theory,* ed. Francois-Xavier Glayzon (Prague: Litteraria Pragensia, 2011), 157–166, Wilson also connects David Lynch with Friedrich Schlegel, arguing that the irony in Lynch's images is similar to the romantic irony Schlegel was famously propagating.
25 Peter Firchow, *Friedrich Schlegel's Lucinde and the Fragments* (Minneapolis: University of Minnesota Press, 1971), 144; Friedrich von Schlegel and Hans Eichner, *Kritische Friedrich Schlegel Ausgabe* II (Paderborn, München, Wien: Ferdinand Schöning Verlag) 1981, 148.

least when he is talking about ideas: It consists of compressed thoughts, sometimes hard to understand, often ambiguous but also precise.

The fragment is an exciting, contradictory, short written form. It is exciting precisely because it is contradictory. It questions coherence and totality at the same time as it constitutes an 'open totality'.[26] The fragment is a totality at the same time as it denies totality. It blurs boundaries and draws attention to boundaries. It is at once a part and a whole, it 'combines completion and incompletion within itself',[27] just like the whole is never closed and finished. Or as put by French philosopher and literary theorist Maurice Blanchot; what the romanticists sought was a form that was neither closed nor open, 'a search for a new form of fulfilment that mobilizes – renders mobile – the whole, even while interrupting it in various ways'.[28]

The following is not an exercise in Schlegel. Neither is it a literature review or an overview of the thinking on the fragment by early German Romanticism. I have picked out some of Schlegel's fragments, which explicitly address the fragment as *a textual form* and *a way of thinking aesthetically.* Moreover, I include contemporary writing on the fragment, primarily from literary studies and philosophy.

Danish literary scholar Jesper Gulddal suggests that aphorisms are short and pithy formulations, in contrast to fragments, which are open and incomplete and more seamlessly included in a larger whole.[29] Schlegel's fragments combine the two forms. Many of them were short and pithy, many were quite long, but his aim was that a fragment should point towards the ideal whole, which to German romanticism was Antiquity. Yet, again, at the same time Schlegel wanted to rethink the understanding of this whole, which he rephrased as never-ending and never definitive but, in a sense, always in the process of becoming, like he writes in the *Athenaeum* Fragment 116 about poetry in general: 'The romantic kind of poetry is still in the state of becoming; that, in fact, is its real essence: that it should forever be becoming and never be perfected'.[30] American literary scholar Peter Firchow emphasizes that the *Critical Fragments* and the *Athenaeum* Fragments differ to the extent that the *Critical Fragments* more resemble singular disparate aphorisms, whereas the *Athenaeum Fragments* create an inner network, in

---

26 Danielle Follett, "*Tout et N'importe Quoi:* The Total Artwork and the Aesthetics of Chance" in *The Aesthetics of the Total Artwork: on Borders and Fragments*, ed. Anke Finger and Danielle Follet (Baltimore: The Johns Hopkins University Press, 2011).
27 Jean-Luc Nancy and Philippe Lacoue-Labarthe, *The Literary Absolute. The Theory of Literature in German Romanticism* (New York: State University of New York Press, 1988 [1978]), 50.
28 Blanchot, "The Athenaeum", 171.
29 Jesper Gulddal, "Indledning" in *Friedrich Schlegel. Athenäum Fragmenter* (Copenhagen: Gyldendal, 2000).
30 Firchow, *Friedrich Schlegel's Lucinde and the Fragments*, 175; Schlegel and Eichner, *Kritische Friedrich Schlegel Ausgabe II*, 183.

which fragments refer to each other.[31] However, what unites the fragments is that they were thought to partly – albeit not radically – contrast the idea so pervasive to the eighteenth-century thinking of a unified rational philosophical system in which everything had its place. As philosopher Olivier Schefer puts it, the fragment 'indicates breaks, fissures and an anti-totality but also the attempt to recompose the whole out of disparate pieces'.[32] Romanticism, in Schefer's take on the fragment, is rethinking wholeness

> out of the fragments instead of trying to inscribe the parts into a preexisting whole. This is clearly not a question of recovering some wholeness after having lost it but rather a question of reconsidering its nature and its form; similarly, the desire for unity that is paradoxically expressed in fragments is not only manifested in the construction of a totality but in the creation of new modes of linking and joining.[33]

Formally, the romantic fragment opposed the universalist thinking at the same time as it supported it, though in a more dispersed and open version – hence the system of assigning consecutive numbers to the fragments; as French philosophers Philippe Lacoue-Labarthe and Jean-Luc Nancy say, 'to write a fragment is to write fragments'.[34] The fragments were very different in length and content, and each of the three collections ended at random. Firchow argues similarly to what Schefer said above: the fragments were not opposing systems, but they were in favour of *another* system: '[T]he fragments are not against systems, they are a substitute for one, a brilliant substitute, for unlike a fully formulated system they need exclude nothing because it is contradictory, or even self-contradictory'.[35]

Schlegel's thinking of the part and the whole, the fragment and the system, was sophisticated. Basically, he wanted to suggest another modern wholeness by writing disparate bits of text that were often contradictory and could not be summarized. A fragment constituted a non-definite whole. In that sense it was always incomplete and vice versa: 'Even the largest system is actually only pure fragment'.[36] Most explicitly, Schlegel wrote in the much-cited *Athenaeum Fragment* 206 that '[a] fragment, like a miniature work of art, has to be entirely isolated from the surrounding world and be complete in itself like a porcupine'.[37] This

---

31 Firchow, *Friedrich Schlegel's Lucinde and the Fragments*.
32 Oliver Schefer, "Variations on Totality: Romanticism and the Total Work of Art" in *The Aesthetics of the Total Artwork: on Borders and Fragments* ed. Anke Finger and Danielle Follet (Baltimore: The Johns Hopkins University Press, 2011), 50.
33 Oliver Schefer, "Variations on Totality", 50.
34 Nancy and Lacoue-Labarthe, *The Literary Absolute*, 43–44.
35 Firchow, *Friedrich Schlegel's Lucinde and the Fragments*, 18.
36 From fragment 930. Schlegel and Eichner, *Kritische Friedrich Schlegel Ausgabe XVI*, 163.
37 Firchow, *Friedrich Schlegel's Lucinde and the Fragments*, 189; Schlegel and Eichner, *Kritische Friedrich Schlegel Ausgabe II*, 197. I have used the English translation of the fragments by Peter Firchow, with a few corrections. I have retained his translation of the German 'Igel' in *Athenaeum Fragment* 206 as "porcupine" even though many other English language texts

definition sounds like the definition of an aphorism. Yet, the use of the metaphor 'porcupine' is quite remarkable. It adds to this seemingly straightforward description of the fragment ('complete in itself' [in sich selbst vollendet]) a sense of ambiguity. The small animal's quilled, pricking fur prevents intrusion but also radiates in all directions well aware of its surrounding; thus it displays an awareness of being in a context. Lacoue-Labarthe and Nancy suggested that the totality of fragments does not make a whole but in a sense replicates a whole and they formulated elegantly the intertwining of the part and the whole: 'Each fragment stands for itself and for that from which it is detached'.[38] This is the way I approach fragments in Lynch's production. I see them as condensed centres of aesthetic and emotional intensity that radiate but also push towards the context of a larger textuality.

In *Athenaeum Fragment* 259 Schlegel described fragments as '[m]arginal glosses to the text of the age'.[39] Gulddal explains that the statement refers to the position of the fragments within the wider intellectual and cultural landscape of the time.[40] Many of the fragments are hard to understand because they comment upon other critical texts and thoughts that were occupying intellectuals (philosophers and literary critics). Therefore, Gulddal warns that it is difficult to capture the entirety of their rich meaning without knowledge of the texts or the discussions they are referring to. Understood as marginal notes, they do not require the completeness Schlegel is suggesting in *Athenaeum Fragment* 206, but they demand the spines or barbs that enable them to actually participate in the text of their time. By being 'marginal glosses to the text of the age', Schlegel saw the fragments as continuing and expanding on the thinking of his time. Even though the quote may seem to place Schlegel and his circle of intellectuals in a position at the margins and diminish the importance of the fragment as a textual form,

---

translate it as 'hedgehog.' The German fragment sounds like this: 'Ein Fragment muss gleich einem kleinen Kunstwerke von der umgebenden Welt ganz abgesondert und in sich selbst vollendet sein wie ein Igel.' Fragment 72 is translated by me, though. The original text goes like this: 'Übersichten des Ganzen wie sie jetzt Mode sind, entstehen, wenn einer alles einzelne übersieht, und dann summiert' See (See Schlegel and Eichner, *Kritische Friedrich Schlegel Ausgabe II, 175)*. Firchow's somewhat imprecise translation reads: 'Surveys of entire subjects of the sort that are now fashionable are the result of somebody surveying the individual items, and then summarizing them'. What Firchow's translation misses is the sarcasm in Schlegel's fragment but also the double meaning of the verb 'übersiehen', which means both 'ignore' and 'survey'. Thus, Firchow's translation does not include the fact that the fragment points at the part as well as the whole. Translations from Schlegel's *Fragmente zur Literatur und Poesie* from German to English are by me.

38 Nancy and Lacoue-Labarthe, *The Literary Absolute*, 44.
39 Firchow, *Friedrich Schlegel's Lucinde and the Fragments*, 199; Schlegel and Eichner, *Kritische Friedrich Schlegel Ausgabe II*, 209.
40 Gulddal, "Indledning".

Schlegel also positioned the fragments as conveyors of prickly, challenging thinking and final words.

Schlegel's thinking of the whole and the part was sophisticated, but it was also ambiguous in the sense that he proposed a new and contemporary, more dynamic and fragmented communicative form and looked for its ideal proponents in classic antiquity. Obviously fragment 812 in *Fragmente zur Literatur und Poesie* proposes a thinking together of the contemporary, modern with the classical: 'The form of the fragments is the pure form of the classical, the progressive and the urban'.[41] In Schlegel's take on the fragment, it was at once an aesthetic form of communication, a mirror of a certain spirit of the age and a comment on his time. The fragments matched the era of burgeoning mass media and periodicals. An issue of a periodical could be filled with as many or as few of the short text form as was fit, and as a short form, the fragment emitted a sense of the here and now. Fragments were comments (political, ironic, literary, philosophical) on contemporary events, and they were quick and transitory. As Justus Fetscher understands it, the early Romanticist fragments 'manifest and record the impulses and tendencies of the present moment'.[42] But they were also meant by Schlegel to provoke reflection.

Since early romanticism, the term has been taken up by writers from Nietzsche to Ernst Bloch, Walter Benjamin, Adorno, Derrida, Blanchot and Roland Barthes.[43] Not least because of Schlegel's reflections upon literature and a 'universal poetry', the term has been related to contemporary discussions on *das Gesamtkunstwerk*.[44] However, I will end this part of the article by referring to Horace Engdahl's thought-provoking fragments about the fragment. Engdahl's text not only touches upon Schlegel and his colleague Novalis but includes more contemporary reflections on the term and advances some pointed notes on the fragment as an oppositional form.[45]

To Horace Engdahl, the fragment is characterized by its ability to 'write in the fissures between culture's fields of enunciation'.[46] To a certain extent, he hereby connects with Schlegel's thinking about writing at the margins. As I read this central passage in his text, he imagines a textual form that can both detect the

---

41 Schlegel and Eichner, *Kritische Friedrich Schlegel Ausgabe XVI*, 154.
42 Fetscher, "Tendency, Disintegration, Decay".
43 Eberhard Ostermann, *Das Fragment. Geschichte einer ästhetischen Idee.* (München: Wilhelm Fink Verlag, 1991).
44 See, for example Anke Finger and Danielle Follet (ed.), *The Aesthetics of the Total Artwork: on Borders and Fragments* ed. (Baltimore: The Johns Hopkins University Press, 2011); Anders V. Munch, *Design as Gesamtkunstwerk: The Art of Transgression.* Copenhagen: Rhodos, 2012).
45 All quotes in the following are from the Swedish text of Engdahl, "Anteckningar", 44–63 and are translated into English by me.
46 Engdahl, "Anteckningar", 55.

cracks in culture's seeming coherence and use these cracks as eruptive spaces to communicate in a different language. Therefore, Engdahl can declare that 'the fragment is there, suddenly, like an event'.[47] It erupts, stands out in its particularity, surprises, and overwhelms. Consequently, Engdahl regards the fragment as an emancipating form: 'a writing outside of generic constraints and a thinking outside of the prescribed [påbjudna] universality'.[48] Fragmentation liberates the mind to Engdahl. 'The fragment is determined to make possible unlimited re-arrangement of the regions of thought'.[49]

In line with Schlegel, Engdahl argues that a fragment seldom stands alone. On the other hand, he calls a series of fragments a contradiction in the sense that using the term 'series' implies some kind of generic similarity as well as a kind of system. All the same, he elegantly solves this contradiction by suggesting that the succession of the parts that together compose a fragment series is not linear. In a way, he says, the fragments 'are separated by an eternity'.[50]

Engdahl looks at the fragment as a sign of the times. The fragment is 'a text that is infected by the disorder of its time, in contrast to the system that is spatial and logical'.[51] Moreover, bearing in mind Engdahl's accentuation of the fragment as a non-genre – an unruly form that can take many different shapes – the fragment denies clues to its reading and should not, by and large, be interpreted. 'The fragment should not be approached through interpretation. Rather, it demands "complement" or "experiment"'.[52] The fragment does not explain, '[i]t is rather a way to respond to [omgås] both the unknown and what is too obvious'.[53] Engdahl makes it clear that the fragment is not a system's or structure's Other. However, what brings together Engdahl's different arguments about the fragment is the idea, inspired by Schlegel, that it challenges our way of thinking of systems and order. Engdahl's text may be summed up as an argument about the instability inherent in order and systems. The fragment is a form that points at the cracks lying dormant in systems. Therefore, by its mere non-form it functions as a challenging undercurrent to the ordering of systems. Not least, the fragment is a means to push forward thinking and reflection both about the unknown, that which lies dormant under the surface, and that which is too well known.

What makes it analytically fruitful to juxtapose scholarly discussions about the fragment and Lynch's works is the shared occupation with the ambivalent relationship between the part and the whole. It is the mutual recognition that the

---

47 Engdahl, "Anteckningar", 44.
48 Engdahl, "Anteckningar", 59.
49 Engdahl, "Anteckningar", 61.
50 Engdahl, "Anteckningar", 45.
51 Engdahl, "Anteckningar", 54.
52 Engdahl, "Anteckningar", 55.
53 Engdahl, "Anteckningar", 61.

whole (a work, a string of thinking, an idea) is never a whole. It is the identical denial of the definite and coherent. It is the occupation with condensed (aesthetic) expressions. In addition to the different media, the difference between Lynch and Schlegel's thoughts of the fragment is that Schlegel was embedded in the occupation with system and entirety in his time and from that position tried to think of system in a different manner. As for Lynch, his work continuously constructs and explores affective 'spaces of otherness'.[54] Worlds without a whole or a centre. The more contemporary thinking about the fragment I have included from Horace Engdahl helps illuminate how Lynch's work, through aesthetics, insists on thinking outside of order and our habitual safety zones. Moreover, it throws light on Lynch's texts as continuously in process. They are not offering themselves to interpretation but to dialogue, dispute, and to the creation of ambiguous feelings of discomfort and awe.

Schlegel lamented somewhat sarcastically that wholes are the result of not paying attention to the parts: 'Those surveys of entire subjects of the sort that are now fashionable are the result of somebody overlooking all the individual items, and then summarizing' (*Athenaeum Fragment* 72). On the other hand, he also wrote in *Gespräch über die Poesie* from approximately the same time:

> It is not possible to understand a part by itself, i.e., it is unwise to want to consider only a part in detail. But the whole is not yet finalized; and therefore, all knowledge of the whole remains only approximation and piecemeal.[55]

Since Schlegel considered neither the whole nor the fragment a finished entity it seems as if he warned against looking in detail at single fragments. David Lynch, on the other hand said in an interview that 'Ideas come in fragments. Each fragment, though, is full'.[56] I go with Lynch's idea of the 'fullness' of the fragment, its "thick" affective atmosphere. I am aware that I now turn away from theorizations of written forms and applies thinking of the written fragment to audio-visual spaces. All the same, my approach to the four Lynch fragments in the following section is, along with Engdahl, to 'complement'. I aim to paraphrase the fragments reflectively instead of subjecting them to 'interpretation' or 'understanding' as Schlegel put it. I thus focus on their aesthetic 'fullness', the way they create condensed atmospheres by way of audio-visuality. Moreover, I shortly describe the context into which the fragments are inserted to consider Schlegel's warning – which simultaneously tells that looking at a fragment in detail does not make it into a whole.

---

54 Jerslev, *Blurred Boundaries*, 256.
55 Schlegel and Eichner, *Kritische Friedrich Schlegel Ausgabe II*, 340.
56 Lynch in Barney, "Inland Empire". Original interview from 2001.

The "Dance for Freedom" and the "Dying Girl" Fragment in *Wild at Heart*

Wild at Heart (1990) is 'largely a film of instants'.[57] This structure goes hand in hand with the film's emphasis on suppressed past incidents, half-memories, and half-truths. Recurrent fragments include the close-ups of fire burning violently behind a broken window. They are brief flashes of memory connected with Lula which are evoked on different occasions but bear no meaning in themselves. They function as eruptions from Lula's archive of hardly comprehensible memories. Fetcher argues that memory is the

> paradigmatic instantiation of fragmentation, of separation into parts, of isolation, of retouching – of the regrouping and distorting reanimation of impressions and means of expression.[58]

Fragmentation is the very structuring principle in this film, and it corresponds formally with the problem that is both Sailor's and Lula's: Lula's fragmented incomplete recollection and lack of knowledge of what happened to her beloved father and her mother's complicity in his death a long time ago; and likewise, Sailor's witnessing of a fire that he could not understand.

However, the fragment of fire, and a broken window, is just one of several recurrent fire fragments in the film that the excessive widescreen images of flames in the title sequence were foreboding. There are also the repeated ultra-close-ups of the burning tip of a cigarette and matches being struck. As magnification has deprived everyday objects of their familiarity and their meaning, they appear as affective outbursts, abstract signifiers of intensity. Other memorable fragments include Sailor's singing of Elvis Presley songs, and the many short, stylized, tableau-like images of Lula and Sailor in dramatic poses. Like muted texts (to refer to Peter Brooks's writing about the tableaux),[59] in which bodies speak affectively instead of by way of dialogue, so do these "body fragments".

Many fragments in *Wild at Heart* are characterized by striking exaggerations, what I would call an aesthetics of excess: excessive magnification, excessive fire, excessive use of the voice and sound, excessive bodily postures, excessive camera angles, excessive expressions of emotion. The fragment at once condenses and spreads intensity across the image, hence creating an affective atmosphere which 'emanate[s] from but exceed[s] the assembling of bodies'.[60]

---

57 Eugenie Brinkema, *The Forms of the Affect* (Durham and London: Duke University Press, 2014).
58 Justus Fetscher, "Tendency, Disintegration, Decay", 53.
59 Peter Brooks, *The Melodramatic Imagination* (New York: Columbia University Press, 1984 [1979]).
60 Anderson, "Affective Atmospheres", 80.

Lula and Sailor's excessive emotional outbursts could even be said to put pressure on the image frame. We see this in a short "dance for freedom" fragment of the couple in the sunset – after Lula has in desperation stopped the car that is meant to take them away from her wicked mother and asked Sailor to find some music on the radio instead of the reports on violent incidents that keep sounding each time she switches channel. The excessive, beautiful, ultra-long shot that concludes the fragment enhances the affective atmosphere in the image: Sailor at last tunes into *Slaughterhouse* performed by metal band *Powermad*. They run into the nearby field, and while the camera slowly lifts high above them, they scream and move violently to the music in the red-yellow light of the descending sun, as if to get the violence Lula heard about out of their bodies. After a short pause, the camera moves further upwards, while the music changes from the diegetic hard rock on the car radio to Richard Strauss's solemn 'Im Abendrot', and Lula and Sailor stop their wild body movements and embrace. After a medium close-up of their passionate embrace in front of the red line of the sunset and the sun reaching the horizon behind them, there is a dissolve to an excessive wide-angle shot of the vast fields and the bending of the planet in the sunset while the violins continue playing the music by Strauss.

If this fragment is 'a marginal gloss to the text of the age' it may be seen as a writing and a lifting of the discomfort in (media) culture. The fragment offers a vision of sublime boundlessness, of freedom and vigorous youthfulness. The final sublime image and the violins' other-worldliness in a sense release Sailor and Lula from their material existence and transport them into a peaceful transcendence where the evil they are fleeing cannot reach them. The fragment moreover draws attention to film as a language that can create visions of limitlessness. Just as the ultra-close-up can magnify matches and cigarettes and provide the well-known with a disturbing unfamiliarity, extreme wide-angle images of limitless nature can create a highly affective atmosphere beyond beautiful. Audio-visual form (framing and camera angle, colour, and music) thus creates the intensity that emanates from the image space by the end of the fragment. The grand super-total makes possible an affective sensibility that transcends Lula and Sailor's emotions. It reminds us of Brian Massumi's thinking on affect which does not belong to certain subjects like emotions and may therefore constitute a more pervasive and condensed, but also ungraspable sensation attached to a space.[61] In this scene, affect spreads across the image as an atmospheric surplus that pushes on the image boundaries. Moreover, the extreme long shot itself is affective.

---

61 Brian Massumi, *Parables for the Virtual. Movement, Affect, Sensation*. (Durham and London: Duke University Press, 2002).

The fragment constitutes a single moment of dizzying freedom and transcendence released from the violent and material here and now. Nonetheless, the fragment partakes of the whole by implying that the beauty in nature and the power of love relate to death. The solemn, melancholic Strauss music adds to the powerful sublimity and sense of freedom a feeling of sorrow and death:[62] the lyrics to the music, which are not audible in the film, end with the following verse: 'Oh weiter stiller Friede!/So tief im Abendrot/Wie sind wir wandermüde - -/ist dies etwa der Tod?' The fragment is 'complete in itself', to quote Schlegel. However, by asking the question 'ist dies etwa der Tod?' 'Im Abendrot' connects with the following fragment from Lula and Sailor's road trip, the incident with the car accident and the dying young woman.

The "dying girl" fragment is a death eulogy. It suddenly appears, as Engdahl says, in the dark, literally out of nowhere, like an event. It is a fragment complete in itself in all its strange difference, constituted as a tableau of darkness and light, red and black, life and death, accompanied by the tone of spinning car wheels and fragile piano and guitar notes. Lula and Sailor are offered no other position than being spectators to this spectacle of another, disrupted order, an event that writes in the margins of contemporary consumer and driving culture. As for the approach to the fragment, which is one of the most memorable moments in the film, again: I 'complement', as Engdahl proposes, seeing it as one significant example of Lynch's powerful writing 'in the fissures between culture's fields of enunciation'.

The fragment starts with an image of the road in the headlights and ends with the car's red rear lights disappearing in the dark. It does not add to the narrative development but contributes with a beautiful and horrible imagery of an almost sacred and totally private other-worldly moment between life and the inevitable death. Sailor wants to take the dying girl to the hospital, but not only is it too late, it is also truly inappropriate, notwithstanding his good intentions. The girl is in a liminal space where she cannot be reached, and her aggressive refusal to allow him to touch her tells him that they already belong to different realms.

Lula and Sailor realize that something has gone awfully wrong when they discover clothes scattered on the road in the dark in front of them and a light on the roadside ahead. When they reach the site of the accident, they pass an invisible threshold to a space of otherness, which they are part of and excluded from at one and the same time. This 'elsewhereness' is emphasized by frail guitar notes from Chris Isaak's *Wicked Game*, which return when they leave the space

---

62 See also Anette Davison, "Up in Flames'. Love, Control and Collaboration in the Soundtrack to *Wild at Heart*" in *The Cinema of David Lynch. American Dreams, Nightmare Visions* ed. Erica Sheen and Anette Davison (London & New York: Wallflower Press, 2004), 119–136.

again. The delicate guitar sounds and the car's approaching and leaving the site of the accident demarcate the fragment.

While they look at the dead bodies lying on the ground beside the overturned cars, a girl comes out of the darkness behind the stems of the Joshua tree (similarly to the way other people emanate from the darkness in Lynch's works). She wears a black top and blue jeans, her lips are red and blood runs down the right part of her face and upper body. The young woman keeps repeating desperately that she cannot find her wallet and all her (credit) cards. 'It was in my pocket!' she cries desperately, putting her hand down her jeans pocket, but 'now my pocket's gone.' Her desperation also includes her mother, whom she repeatedly says will kill her when she finds out that she has lost the wallet.

When she approaches Lula and Sailor, she lifts a short piece of metal thread towards them and says, as if she wanted to explain something, 'this bobby pin'. After she has refused Sailor's help and angrily called out for 'Robert' – like they were in the middle of an everyday quarrel – faint piano tunes sound while she starts scratching her scalp and repeats in a close-up: 'I have this sticky stuff in my hair.' She turns toward Sailor who looks at her sorrowfully, well knowing what she does not seem to (want to) know, and as she falls to the ground, she cries for her hairbrush. In her dying moment, lying on the ground in a medium-close-up, she whispers: 'Get my lipstick. It's in my purse.' With blood running out of her mouth, she seems to be addressing an important moment in everyday life and clinging to life, even in her moment of death: brushing her hair and painting her lips. In another way too, the fragment stages the blurring of boundaries between life and death in this liminal space: the blood and her red lips are exactly the same colour.

Sailor rises from the dead girl and says, 'Let's get out of here, honey.' His remark is an apt expression of this fatal in-between space as an enclosure of otherness in the middle of the vast desert. It also captures the sense of this site as a space, a 'here' they can 'get out of'. The fatal space is demarcated by the overturned cars, the clicking wheels still turning and the headlights still on. Lula and Sailor crossed a threshold to this space, but they are alive and can therefore choose to 'get out of here' again. When Sailor has escorted the crying Lula to the car, he lights a cigarette before he gets into the car. This gesture is an expression of his escape from the uncanny space of death and a wished-for return to everyday normality. However, the cigarette and the matchstick, elsewhere in the film magnified and made strange in ultra close-ups, are also signs of the violence that is the dark side to the everyday in the film.

The dying girl fragment adds to the critical writing on postmodern culture and contributes 'marginal glosses' to its time. In *America*, published in 1986, just a few years before *Wild at Heart* premiered, Jean Baudrillard wrote about speed and the desert as the epitome of America as the scene of simulation: 'Speed creates a space of initiation, which may be lethal; its only rule is to leave no trace behind. Triumph of forgetting over memory, an uncultivated, amnesic intoxication […] driving is a spectacular form of amnesia. Everything is to be discovered, everything to be obliterated'.[63] Indeed, driving is lethal in *Wild at Heart* but in this fragment, it leaves traces behind. Moreover, driving to Lula and Sailor is a spectacular form of amnesia but their surroundings keep pushing in on them, not least here in the desert confronted with the dying girl. In Baudrillard's thinking the desert is a space turned into a hyperreal nothingness, an 'extensive banality'.[64] However, in *Wild at Heart*, the desert is the scene of a fatal car accident.[65] Yet, this elegy to death is also, in a paradoxical way, a hymn to the life the dying girl clings to when she asks for her lipstick. By contrast, Lula's wicked mother Marietta's red lips are the lips of a black angel. Marietta is closer to a made-up corpse than the dying girl is. The "dying girl" fragment is surrounded by two scenes of evil: crime and death involving Lulas' mother whom they are fleeing. Thus, the context of the fragment contributes to also making this elegy into a tribute to the rituals of ordinary beauty which life consists of.

The Las Vegas Fragment and the Floating Cube Fragment in *Twin Peaks: The Return*

From *Wild at Heart*, I now turn to two examples of the destabilizing and defamiliarization of a delimited rule-governed space in *Twin Peaks: The Return*. The series has, since its premiere on Showtime on May 21, 2017, continuously been referred to as 'fragmented'.[66] This regards its incoherent narrative structure – 'layers of stories within stories within stories that blend and fragment in unexpected ways'[67] – its weird spatial leaps and temporal discontinuities, its stories that do not offer closure and characters which multiply: *doppelgängers* or *tulpas* – artificially constructed replicates/replicants. Altogether, there is an abundance of split subjectivities in *Twin Peaks: The Return.* The fragmented series and its many fragments create an image of a confusing, incoherent, and impossible to

---

63 Jean Baudrillard, *America* (London and New York: Verso, 1999 [1986]), 6–9.
64 Baudrillard, *America,* 9.
65 I have also written about Baudrillard and the desert in relation to *Lost Highway* (See Anne Jerslev, "Beyond Boundaries. David Lynch's *Lost Highway*" in *The Cinema of David Lynch. American Dreams, Nightmare Visions* ed. Erica Sheen and Anette Davison (London & New York: Wallflower Press, 2004), 151–165.) Just like in *Wild at Heart*, the desert and the darkness coalesce in *Lost Highway* into a non-space in which natural order dissolves.
66 See Antonio Sanna (ed.), *Critical Essays on* Twin Peaks: The Return (Cham, Switzerland: Palgrave Macmillan, 2019).
67 Timothy William Galow, "From *Lost Highway* to *Twin Peaks:* Representations of Trauma and Transformation in Lynch's Late Work" in *Critical Essays on* Twin Peaks: The Return ed. Antonio Sanna (Cham, Schwitzerland: Palgrave Macmillan), 212.

understand contemporary world, and this incoherent structure can, as suggested by Timothy Galow 'be viewed either as fragments or as supplements of an elusive whole'.[68] Simultaneously, the series refrains from offering a unifying point of view from where to comprehend this fragmentation, which is what makes viewing such a frightening and thrilling, awesome and exhausting experience at one and the same time.

What I call the "Las Vegas fragment" at the beginning of Episode 4 in *Twin Peaks: The Return* takes place in the slot machine hall in a Las Vegas casino. The casino is presented as a miniature version of the capitalist system. However, the fragment also constitutes the gaming hall as a mirror of the fragility of such a system, once a radically disturbing force gains entrance to it. The fragment opens with agent Dale Cooper turned into confused insurance agent Dougie Jones going from the outside through the revolving doors to the guarded inside of a casino. Dougie has difficulties understanding the revolving doors, which, of course, is a sign of his mental state but also draws attention to the door to the casino as a symbolic threshold. This *other space* is utterly strange to the confused man. He creates total chaos in the slot machine hall by disturbing the monetary logic – the distribution of the accumulation and spending of money between two distinct actors, the owners and the players, respectively.

Baudrillard argues that the Las Vegas space and its gaming enclosures have 'a desert form, inhuman, uncultured, initiatory, a challenge to the natural economy of value, a crazed activity on the fringes of exchange'.[69] Dougie is the innocent fool who disturbs the already 'crazed activity' in this capitalist hall of mirrors. Apparently, he can detect which machines give immediate jackpot and he helps an old bag lady choose the right machines. Involuntarily he rebels against the exploitative system built into the machines and by demolishing its logic he turns the gaming space into an unruly inferno of coins rolling and noises from the jackpots (which, significantly, sound like alarms). Dougie does not understand the space he interrupts and leaves the coins in the slot machine each time he has hit the jackpot. However, his unruly presence creates a breach in an exploitative system – and its assistants see to it that he is expelled from the gaming space by throwing him out of the same door he entered. Just like the "dying girl" fragment, the casino space is turned into a space of otherness and the fragment constitutes an audio-visual moment of disruption.

As for the other-worldly fragment in the 'Mauve Zone'[70] in *Twin Peaks: The Return*, it forms as a journey into a fantastic space. At the opening of Episode 3,

---

68 Galow, "From *Lost Highway* to *Twin Peaks*", 208.
69 Baudrillard, *America*, 108.
70 This place is called the Mauve Zone, according to the index entry in Sanna (ed). 2019. See also https://twinpeaks.fandom.com/wiki/Purple_sea.

Cooper lands on a cube, which, as it turns out, is floating somewhere in between the vast ocean and the immense starlit space. Additionally, we meet the eerie Naido, with her eyes stitched together. The sublime feeling of awe that this fragment invites is caused by a range of distortions of scale, the use of colour (nuances of lilac and mauve primarily), and of a kind of stop motion technique, in which tiny fragments of movements are briefly repeated, accompanied by a shuffling sound, as if moving was somehow impossible. Additionally, the fragment uses an extraordinary boundary-blurring aesthetics that linger somewhere in between drawn, painted, and filmed images. There are unexpected and awe-inspiring long shots, and finally, this weird and breathtaking fragment is almost wordless.

The fragment starts like Episode 2 ended, Cooper whirling involuntarily through dark air. Everything shakes, images are blurred, Cooper at times seems to whirl into the camera, and the surrounding darkness is filled with white spots and lines. Then his face slowly turns lilac as he is forced to pass through a lilac foamy substance that keeps multiplying. There is a cut to a complete opposite figure – a massive lilac surface that fills the entire screen and looks like a segment of a large building, constructed of metal or concrete. After a few seconds without anything happening on this seemingly flat, lilac surface, Cooper falls downwards into the image and lands, presumably, on a ledge. This movement in the otherwise static image finally confers upon the strange structure an idea of scale. It is huge apparently, as Cooper looks like a tiny figure in front of the building. When he subsequently looks out and downwards from the ledge, he sees far below him, as do we, the vast, lilac ocean under the slightly shining dark lilac sky. Like in a dystopian science fiction novel, it feels as if the lilac darkness will never disappear, and the building is completely isolated.

Upon entering the dark room, which has a vaulted ceiling and light coming from a fireplace and a few lamps – as if he had entered a crypt under a castle – Cooper catches sight of a woman, whose eyes are stitched together with pieces of skin and flesh. She is a porcelain doll-looking woman in a shining purple velvet dress who seems unable to talk except for some faint groaning. When Cooper approaches her, they both seem to be caught by the stopping of time in a series of split seconds. It is as if time collapses, which makes it hard for them to move towards each other in this weird space in which usual time-space coordinates seem to be out of order.

A long shot shows the cavernous, yet marvellous, room and the bewildered-looking Cooper talks for the first and last time during the fragment's duration of around nine minutes. He asks, just as the viewer would like to know: 'Where is this? Where are we?' Notably, Cooper does not say, 'Where am I?' as if he did not feel like an 'I' placed involuntarily in a strange space, as if the space might engulf what 'I' there was. Neither does he say, 'What is this?' The question he poses accentuates the importance of space to the constitution of the fragment but also that space is contextually defined. It also accentuates that the fragment's space is remarkable in some – mysterious, unfamiliar, powerful – way and is distinctive by its condensed atmosphere. The lack of dialogue in this extended fragment furthermore accentuates the strangeness and 'elsewhereness' of the space.

Cooper may get some sort of an answer as the blinded woman forces him to follow her out of a door and up a ladder. She is seen opening a hatch, and in the next shot we see the hatch being opened from the outside and the woman stepping off the ladder. What is revealed in this shot is Cooper and the woman standing on top of a dark cube floating in the middle of the starlit space. So, the answer to Cooper's question seems to be 'Somewhere'. There is no spatial anchoring to the cube, no limit to the space in which it floats. The image of the small cube with the two persons on top of it, so much smaller than its inner scale seemed to suggest, therefore yields at once a frightening sense of boundlessness and an awesome sense of the unimaginable. So, maybe a more correct answer to the question would be 'Nowhere'.

After Cooper's dizzying fall through air, we first saw an extraordinary image of a wall that seems to continue far beyond the image frame. The second grandiose and vertiginous view in this fragment was of Cooper looking at the dark waves far below him, which confirmed the feeling of the immensity of the construction on which he stood. Finally, the third sublime shot adds another surprising and awesome view regarding not only "where" but also "what". In contrast to what we would have expected, the woman and Cooper are not stepping into another room in a building firmly standing on the ground but are out on the top of a metallic cube, which floats in the dark space and is dimly lit by the stars or a moon. In contrast to the first view, which provided an impression of a huge structure, in front of which Cooper became tiny, the cube from which the camera in this first view slightly tracks away is small and can hardly make room for the two on the top. The next medium close-up shows the slight bumping of the cube in deep, dark space while Cooper and the woman try to stay erect by holding on to a metal bar.

This outside shot forces the viewer to reconsider the previous part from the inside of the cube. Ocean has been supplanted by space, large scale by small scale, grounding by floating, as if the cube were a spaceship advancing on its slow route to infinity. This sense of sublime spatial limitlessness is accentuated when the woman pulls a lever on the side of a large, strange "thing", which stands on the top of the cube, resulting in the electrification of the "thing", the waves of which send the woman catapulting out and down into the vast dark in which she disappears.

If the fragment is defined by being at once part of a whole and 'complete in itself', it stops here, after approximately nine minutes, with the blinded woman credited as Naido whirling through the dark – just like Cooper did in the beginning.

While the Las Vegas fragment and the dying girl fragment may be seen as 'marginal glosses to the text of the age', as Schlegel put it, I regard this fragment as creating more of a *perceptual disturbance*. It adds to the way Lynch's works in general disturb the habitual, forcing us to see and hear differently, to challenge, for example, habits of perceiving and making meaning of space and its sounds. Richard Martin says in his book about architecture in Lynch's work that '[w]hile watching Lynch's films, spatial awareness is both demanded and undermined'.[71] This is what this fragment does. It challenges our sense of space and of spatial proportions. In so doing, it does not add to a story but shakes our perceptual habits – this is the reason for its presence in the episode.

Conclusion

The importance of Lynch's work to me is that it denies straight-out totalities and coherence. It denies what is pleasant and easily consumable by often pushing on several sensory registers at the same time, maintaining the unresolvable and enigmatic and creating powerful eruptions of condensed atmospheres in which sound and images may be mutually enforcing or create opposing image- and soundscapes. Taking the fragment as the overall analytical approach to Lynch's works implies denying the text as a puzzle in which any single piece only gives meaning when put in its one right place. Even though finding a solution to a Lynch puzzle may be satisfying (for example the intriguing *Mulholland Drive* (2001) narrative), thinking about Lynch's works as fragments offers the possibility of highlighting the disruptive force of aesthetics and entering powerful and intriguing affective spaces, in which anything can happen, in which the totality is lost from view and where one can get lost in architectures of boundlessness.

In Lynch, fragments create atmospheres of intensity, which may emanate from the characters, but characters are just as often merely parts of concentrated audio-visual spatialities characterized by affect, by disorder, by being out of place, and, paradoxically, by a sense of limitlessness which creates even more intensity when captured within the fragment form. Hence, Lynch's fragments can be said to experiment with the visualization of limitlessness and how to push audio-visuality beyond the narrow bounds of the frame.

The textually challenging and aesthetically powerful in the fragment is based on the way it formally contradicts established dichotomies – its uneasy lingering in-between the part and the whole, at once a disparate part of a whole and a whole. Similarly, the whole is always incomplete and yet a whole. It is a stand-

---

71 Richard Martin, *The Architecture of David Lynch* (London, New Delhi, New York & Sydney: Bloomsbury Press, 2014), 2.

alone textual form and yet it does not stand alone. In the Schlegel fragments I have discussed and in Horace Engdahl's radical take on the fragment as emancipating, the fragment challenges system and order. Thus, its writing at the margins, as Schlegel put it, is a powerful intervention in culture and may even effect disruptions in culture. In Lynch's challenging audio-visual works, fragments perform powerful interventions in culture by aesthetic means.

Lynch's fragments are aesthetically and emotionally powerful; they are 'full' although not finished entities. The fragments' creation of unfamiliar, affective spaces and condensed atmospheres point at the disorder in culture and many of them offer experiences of discomfort and awe at the same time. They 'write' in the 'fissures between culture's fields of enunciation' to quote Horace Engdahl once more. Bringing a concept dating back to early romanticism, such as the fragment into conversation with works of a contemporary filmmaker like David Lynch adds fresh insight to these works simultaneously with bringing to our attention how romanticist thinking reverberates in corners of even contemporary audio-visual culture. Reading Lynch through the fragment can thus shed a different light on his bold disruptions of (narrative) order and system and his creation of spaces of aesthetic surplus and intensity.

Review

Mythology and Nation Building: N. F. S. Grundtvig and His European Contemporaries

Edited by Sophie Bønding, Lone Kølle Martinsen, and Pierre-Brice Stahl
Aarhus: Aarhus University Press, 2021
384 pp., 399,95 DKK

The anthology addresses the use of pre-Christian myths in European nation-building during the long 19th century, with writer, pastor, and politician N. F. S. Grundtvig (1783–1872) as its point of departure. The aim of the publication is twofold: Firstly, it demonstrates how cultural and political utilizations of mythologies, especially Old Norse and Germanic ones, were a European phenomenon, which calls for a comparative perspective. Secondly, the anthology highlights the importance of Grundtvig by establishing a dialogue between him and contemporary writers from Denmark, Germany, England, etc. Due to his extensive and idiosyncratic writing, the study of Grundtvig has been a daunting task for scholars, who, as stated in the book's introduction, tend to present him as a unique thinker or 'lone rider' with no or minor significant equals. While this approach has led to insightful works across fields of Literature, History, Philology, and Theology, it has nevertheless resulted in a lack of comparative studies. By successfully situating one of the most famous Danish writers in a larger, European context, this anthology thereby offers an important contribution to both Romantic and Grundtvigian studies.

In the introduction, editors Sophie Bønding, Lone Kølle Martinsen, and Pierre-Brice Stahl present the 19th century as the period of 'becoming' in Europe, referring to Paul-Henri Mallet, Johann Gottfried Herder, and Thomas Percy, whose work in the 18th century rehabilitated the former negative stereotype of the pre-Christian pagans in Northern Europe. The book operates with a broad concept of myth and/or mythology: Myths refer to stories about superhuman agents, such as gods, but are also interpreted as forms of convictions or credos. Most importantly, the question of historical accuracy regarding the 'original' myth is irrelevant. Rather, the contributors focus on the national-oriented adaptations or recreations of folklore and written sources concerning mythology, particularly the Norse myths from medieval sources. As such, the anthology situates itself among the interdisciplinary fields of reception, memory, and medievalism studies, all of which have experienced a growing interest during the last couple of decades. The publication is also a valuable addition to the comparative turn within nationalism studies, as it demonstrates the advantages of a more cross-national approach to nationalism and understands culture as inseparable from nationalism, not a by-product. This approach is reminiscent of that of former anthologies such as *Northbound*[1] and *Romantic Norths*[2] since they all examine the cultural exchanges behind the re-evaluation and mythologization of Northern Europe.

All 12 chapters fall into three sections: "Theoretical Perspectives" provides a historical and conceptual framework for readers unfamiliar with the rediscovery of mythological texts, and the contributions from Joep Leerssen, Thomas Mohnike, and Katrine Frøkjær Baunvig complement each other convincingly. Leerssen and Mohnike amplify the importance of national institutions and global networks, both crucial factors in the foundation of comparative mythology and philology. While Mohnike focuses on the geographical space of Old Norse myths, Leerssen and Baunvig emphasize how the romantic writers did not believe the myths themselves in a literal sense. They instead regarded myths as narrative archetypes with inherent aesthetic as well as educational values, that made them express a specific national character. As Baunvig ads, this new attitude towards mythology reflects the writers' effort to re-enchant society and oppose its naturalistic and secularized worldview.

The second section, "N. F. S. Grundtvig and His Danish Contemporaries", begins with an informative chapter by Sune Auken, who links Grundtvig's general views on Old Norse mythology and Danish identity to his overall hermeneutics and understanding of people and history. Following Auken and drawing on memory scholars Jan Assmann and Renate Lachmann, Sophie Bønding demonstrates Grundtvig's attempt to re-mythologize a modern and secularized Denmark. The section's final contributors, Lone Kølle Martinsen and Alderik Blom, expand Grundtvig's authorship by comparing him to writers B. S. Ingemann and Adam Oehlenschläger as well as the philologist Rasmus Rask. Martinsen presents a historical concept analysis focusing on gender, as she interprets the romantic myth of the Nordic, independent woman as an integral part of contemporary concepts of nation, people, and democracy. By adding Valkyries, shieldmaidens, and Amazons in their works, authors strengthened the new term for women, 'kvinder', in the latter half of the 19th century and laid a foundation for other future discussions about gender equality. Blom's chapter addresses Rask's rationalistic and historical approach to Old Norse sources as well as his antipathy towards poetical treatments of the same manuscripts, and how his pioneering work thus separates him from many contemporary colleagues.

---

[1] Karen Klitgaard Povlsen (ed.), *Northbound – Travels, Encounters, and Constructions 1700–1830* (Aarhus: Aarhus University Press, 2007).

[2] Cian Duffy (ed.), *Romantic Norths: Anglo-Nordic Exchanges, 1770–1842* (Berlin: Springer, 2017).

The third and final section, "European Contemporaries", expands the anthology's comparative perspective with case studies from Iceland, Sweden, England, and the Netherlands: Jón Karl Helgason gives a comparative analysis of Jónas Hallgrímsson's poem *Ísland* (1835), which laments the loss of Iceland's golden age of proto-democratic values and harmony. Paula Henrikson studies Per Adam Wallmark's *The Souliotes* (1826), a historical play based on the Greek War of Independence and a fine example of how writers interpreted Nordic myths in the light of Greek mythology, as they both shared admirable traditions and were useful for topical discussions about political autonomy. Heather O'Donoghue explains William Morris' fascination with Old Norse literature in the light of Britain's urge to establish a cultural connection to Germany and Scandinavia as alternatives to the empire's French and Norman legacy. Stephanie Barczewski outlines Arthurian nationalism in a historical perspective, beginning with the Hundred Years' War and ending with Brexit. In both cases, Arthurian legends are meant to boost a sense of national identity and exceptionalism, supporting the myth of a (lonely) Britain against a continental (and Catholic) Europe. Finally, Simon Halink presents a case study of the artists in the Oosterbek School and their sublime and gothic paintings of the forest known as Oaks of Wodan (*Wodanseiken*). As Halink writes, the need to mythologize the Dutch landscape was heavily inspired by Jacob Grimm's *Deutsche Mythologie* (1835), and culminated in the controversial *The Oera Linda Book*, published in the 1860s. Much like James Macpherson's Ossian 100 years before, the book offered a foundational, but fictional, myth intended to strengthen the national sense of identity.

While each chapter can be read separately, the tripartite composition creates a sense of dialogue between all contributors. The anthology provides essential material for Grundtvigian scholars, who wish to understand the wider context for the author, whose texts almost exclusively call for a contextual reading. However, it would have been interesting to integrate some of Grundtvig's views on Greek mythology to supplement the book's dominant focus on Old Norse and Germanic myths. While such an addition would require a more elaborate chapter on Grundtvig's complex poetics and reflections on nationalism, it could also expand some of the discussions in the "European Contemporaries"-section, especially that of Henrikson's. Most contributors (7 out of 12) have a background in literature and/or language studies, but the anthology can easily attract readers from interdisciplinary fields, including medievalists. With its focus on Grundtvig and European contemporaries, the anthology handles its broad topics "nationalism" and "mythology" in a well-thought, comprehensive way, and its comparative method brings out new and overlooked aspects of well-known writers.

Lea Grosen Jørgensen
Aarhus University

About the Authors

Emil Månsson is a PhD canditate in philosophy at the University of Iceland, with the project Embodied Critical Thinking (ECT). Emil holds degrees in literature (BA) and phenomenology and philosophy of mind (MA), both from the University of Copenhagen. His PhD thesis is entitled "Living Well in a Dying World: On Humanity's Responsibility for Itself" and fuses ecophenomenology and critical phenomenology with extinction studies, deep adaptation, new materialism, and the project of ecosocialism, as well as non-canonical, non-colonial perspectives.

University of Iceland, Department of History and Philosophy
Sæmundargata 10, 101 Reykjavik
emm19@hi.is

Robert W. Rix is Associate Professor and Director of Research at the University of Copenhagen. He is widely known for his many publications on the eighteenth and nineteenth centuries, in areas such as politics, religion, language, nationalism, and print culture. Rix has published on William Blake, the Nordic influence on English Romanticism as well as the monograph *The Barbarian North in Medieval Imagination. Ethnicity, Legend, and Literature* (Routledge, 2014). His forthcoming book on the history of Greenland will be published by Cambridge University Press and is entitled *The Vanished Settlers: In Search of a Legend and Its Legacy.*

University of Copenhagen, Department of English, Germanic and Romance Studies
Emil Holms Kanal 6, 2300 Copenhagen S.
rjrix@hum.ku.dk

Anthony Apesos is a professor in the fine arts department at Lesley University, Cambridge, MA. He was the founding director of the MFA program in visual arts at Lesley. He is the author of *Anatomy for Artists: A New Approach to Discovering, Learning and Remembering the Body* and is currently at work on a book on William Blake's depictions of the Last Judgment. Among his published articles are several on self-portraiture in narrative paintings, including Titian's *Flaying of Marsyas* and Caravaggio's *Taking of Christ*. Apesos has shown his paintings in many one person and group exhibitions.

Lesley University
29 Everett St, Cambridge MA 02138
aapesos@lesley.edu
Webpage: apesos.com

Sveinn Yngvi Egilsson is professor of Icelandic literature at the University of Iceland. Among his publications are volumes on nineteenth-century literature, ranging from the re-publications studies (*Arfur og umbylting*, Tradition and Revolution, 1999) to eco-criticism (*Náttúra ljóðsins*, The Nature of Poetry, 2014). He has also edited the works of nineteenth-century writers such as Jónas Hallgrímsson (co-editor of the four-volume *Ritverk Jónasar Hallgrímssonar*, The Works of Jónas Hallgrímsson) and Gísli Brynjólfsson (*Ljóð og laust mál*, Poetry and Prose, 2003), as well as the medieval Njal's Saga (*Brennu-Njálssaga: Texti Reykjabókar*, The Story of Burnt Njáll: The Reykjabók Text, 2003/2004).

University of Iceland
Árnagarður-419, Sturlugata 1, 101 Reykjavík, Iceland
sye@hi.is

Helena Bergmann is Associate Professor of English literature at the University of Borås. She attained her doctoral degree at the University of Gothenburg with a thesis on the roles of women in the 19th century industrial novel. Most of her research has since focussed on 18th century women's writing, in particular on the works of Mary Hays.

University of Borås, Department of Education
Allégatan 1, 503 32 Borås, Sweden
helena.bergmann@hb.se

About the Authors

Anne Jerslev is Professor of Film and Media Studies at the Department of Communication, University of Copenhagen. Since her first monograph, *David Lynch: I vores øjne* (Frydenlund, 1990) (translated into German as *David Lynch: Mentale Landschaften* (Passagen Verlag, 1995) she has published numerous articles about David Lynch in Danish, Scandinavian and International journals and volumes. Her latest publication is *David Lynch: Blurred Boundaries* (Palgrave Macmillan 2021).

University of Copenhagen, Department of Communikation
Karen Blixens Plads 8, 2300 Copenhagen S
jerslev@hum.ku.dk

Lea Grosen Jørgensen is a research assistent at Comparative Literature and Rhetorics at Aarhus University, where she also defended her PhD. Her dissertation was part of the research project *Medievalism in Danish Romantic Literature* (2018–2021) and focused on the reception of Old Norse literature in the writings of Adam Oehlenschläger (1779–1850) and N. F. S. Grundtvig (1783–1872). Although her research concerns Romantic medievalism, she has a great interest in contemporary medievalism, having written about the series Vikings (2013–2020) and held both public speeches and guest lectures about modern Viking music and J. R. R. Tolkien's influence on popular perceptions of the Middle Ages and fantasy fiction. She currently teaches 19th century literature at Aarhus University.

Aarhus University, Comparative Literature and Rhetorics
Langelandsgade 139, bygning 1580, 136, 8000 Aarhus C
leagj@cc.au.dk